B.R.M.

(Bathroom Reading Material)

for Youth Workers

B.R.M.

(Bathroom Reading Material)

for Youth Workers

Jeremy Halstead

RESOURCE *Publications* · Eugene, Oregon

B.R.M. (BATHROOM READING MATERIAL) FOR YOUTH WORKERS

Resource Publications
An Imprint of Wipf and Stock Publishers
199 W. 8th Ave., Suite 3
Eugene, OR 97401

www.wipfandstock.com

ISBN 13: 978-1-4982-0322-7

Manufactured in the U.S.A.   12/01/2014

Dedicated to my wife and ministry partner, Rhonda, who has journeyed with me these past twenty years. Thank you for all you have done along the way; all that you are currently doing; and all that you have yet to do. You have truly made me look good, perform well, and stay strong for our God and for our students. I love you.

For all of the youth workers who labor beside me and who are coming behind me: may God bless the work of your hands. Stay true to God, to your calling, and to your students.

Contents

CONTENTS

Introduction

I know it is a strange name; but everyone uses the bathroom, and most people read while doing so, so why not read about what you love and are involved in: youth ministry.

I believe youth ministry can be, and needs to be, simple.

I wrote this book based upon my ideas, experiences, stories, victories, and failures during my nineteen years in full time church youth ministry. I wrote it as a book that I would want to read: short chapters and simple to understand.

I also wrote it as a tool for you to use. You can read it from beginning to end, or just open it to any page, as there is no rhyme or reason to the order of my chapters. As you read I hope that you are inspired to try something new, are educated with fresh information and ideas, and equipped to implement what you have read immediately in to your ministry.

My desire is that you find my book interesting, enjoyable, encouraging, and educational. May God bless you and your ministry.

Impromptu Theater

One of my favorite ways to tell a Bible story is through what I call Impromptu Theater.

In order to host your own Impromptu Theater, first choose your Bible story. Count how many characters are involved (including all animals and inanimate objects). Without telling your students what they will be doing, ask for that number of volunteers. Pull these students aside and assign each of them a character, animal or object.

Introduce the story to the rest of the group, and tell them that as you read the story the volunteers will act it out. If there are speaking parts in the story, make sure that the volunteers deliver their lines (after you have read them, the actors will deliver them in character). Stress to your thespians to truly become their part.

If at all possible, include the rest of the group (the audience) by having them cheer the heroes and boo the villains; or say the lines of the crowd if there are any in the story.

The beauty of using Impromptu Theater is that there is little to no prep work; any student can pull off a part in the play; it is more fun than just reading the words on a page, and it truly brings the story to life.

Parental Consent Form

No matter if you are taking your students on a trip across the country by plane, train or automobile, or if you are just taking them across town for a round of putt-putt, have them and their parents sign a Parental Consent Form (P.C.F.).

Create a master P.C.F. and save it to your hard drive. Print one off for each student in your ministry and have their parents fill in the needed information. Type each student's information in to a P.C.F., and save a file for each student. Prior to each event change the date(s) and the event, print off a copy for all attending students, and have it signed by both the students and the parents.

Remind parents to keep you updated on any changes that need to be made to the master copy for their particular student.

Be sure to shred every printed copy after each event is over.

I have enclosed a sample P.C.F. at the end of this book, see Appendix B.

First Aid Kit

Have a doctor, nurse or other health care professional in your church assemble a First Aid Kit for your ministry. The amount of supplies needed will be determined by the size of your group. Check expiration dates annually and update your supplies.

Make sure that your adult volunteers, your students, and their parents are aware that you have a First Aid Kit and that it is available on all outings and trips. If possible, have an adult trained in the medical field chaperone each event, outing and trip.

Include a line item in your annual budget to fund your First Aid Kit.

I have included a list of supplies that you may want to include in your First Aid Kit at the end of the book, see Appendix A.

Chick Bag

Have one of your female adult volunteers assemble a bag that contains everything a young girl might need while on either a day outing or a week long journey out of state. Use a purse for your Chick Bag to conceal the contents and to help relieve any possible embarrassment.

Make sure that your adult volunteers, your female students, and their parents are aware that you have a Chick Bag and that it is available on all outings and trips.

Things to include in your Chick Bag are:

- Hair berets
- Hair ties
- Underwear
- Tampons
- Feminine pads
- Midol
- Fingernail clippers & file

Joys & Sorrows

Joys are the good things that are happening in a student's life; the blessings God is giving them and the things they want to praise Him for. Sorrows are the sad things that are happening in a student's life; the struggles they are facing and the things they need to pray about.

Joys & Sorrows can be shared in a variety of ways: in a large group, in small groups, or in pairs. Joys & Sorrows can be used during any youth gathering: during Sunday school, or on Wednesday nights, as part of a weekend get-a-way, in a hotel room, at summer camp, or on a winter retreat . . .

There are huge benefits to maintaining the same Joys & Sorrows groups with the same adult leaders for the course of a school year. There are also benefits to forming groups as seventh graders and keeping these groups together through high school graduation; however, this model also means that groups are of the same age, which can be a negative when building a youth family.

I have used Joys & Sorrows on a regular basis during my Wednesday night youth programs. I have also incorporated them on trips, usually in the evenings during devotions.

Fundraising

Fundraising is necessary for most youth leaders and ministries. My suggestion is to find a handful of successful, enjoyable, high profit fundraisers and learn to do them well, then make them annual events.

I also suggest that you set up accounts for each of your students. You can either set up an account for each family, or for each student. In my current ministry our accounts are set up as family accounts.

You can divide the profits from your fundraisers by one of two ways: by the hour or by the piece. Here is how these two ways work: if you host a sweetheart dinner in February, then the students and parents who work are paid an hourly wage; if you sell nuts and candy in the fall, then the students are paid by the number of bags they sell.

When you do a fundraiser that is divided by an hourly wage, always include an extra worker: the general fund. By giving your general fund an equal share you insure future funds for your ministry.

Make your fundraising a teachable moment to both your students and your church by tithing on your earnings. Every fall, after we run a concession stand at an annual auction I like to tithe the next day by sticking a roll of one dollar bills in the plate. Since I sit on the front pew of the church, most of the congregation gets to see our big fat tithe (plus it is fun just knowing that the ushers have to unroll the bills and count each one).

Early in my ministry career I had a good friend who worked in the food service industry tell me that food will be my best fundraiser, simply because everyone needs to eat. He also told me to sell a quality product, with a generous portion, for a fair price, and I would make money.

Our annual fundraisers are:

February—sweetheart dinner with grilled steak or chicken, salad, green beans, baked potatoes, and dessert

Easter—handmade quarter pound chocolate covered candy eggs in the following flavors: Peanut Butter, Cherry, Coconut, and Butter Cream

April—luncheon for the Red Hat Chapters in our county. The menu is determined according to their theme

July—direct traffic and parking at our county fair. We work four hours a night for eight nights

September—run the only concession stand at a local tree nursery's annual auction. This is an all-day affair, where we serve breakfast, lunch and dinner. Our workers are scheduled in four hour shifts

October—nut and candy sale through a local dealer

November—being in Ohio, home of the Buckeyes, we use our Peanut Butter egg recipe to make candy buckeyes and sell them prior to the Ohio State vs Michigan football game

Throughout the year as other fundraising opportunities arise we do our best to capitalize on them as well.

Curriculum

To be honest, I am not a fan of off the shelf, out of the box curriculum. The simple fact is that the authors who write such curriculums are not specifically writing for you, for your students, for your ministry, or for your specific setting.

If you do use out of the box curriculum I suggest that you research the curriculum, the author, and the content before purchasing. I once ordered a four part lesson from a nationally known youth pastor based on his name and the subject matter. It was the worst piece of curriculum I have ever purchased.

I strongly suggest that you cut and paste (and maybe even re-write or re-work) the curriculum to better fit and serve your students and ministry. This is exactly what I had to do with the above mentioned lessons in order to make it work.

I also caution you to choose carefully how you spend your curriculum budget. Too many times I have witnessed eager youth leaders attending a youth ministry conference walk into the makeshift book store with their church credit card and walk out with their hands and arms literally overflowing with books, dvds and curriculum. My fears are that they have just blown their entire budget; that they will never have time to teach all of the curriculum that they just bought; and, sadly, that they will repeat the same behavior at the next convention they attend.

Instead of buying curriculum, try writing your own. If you are a good writer and teacher, that is great; if not, start by writing one lesson, then work your way up to three and four lessons in a series. The benefit to writing your own is that you know your students, your ministry context, and your teaching style. What you write never has to be published; it just has to meet the needs of your students and of your ministry.

Sunday School Teachers

If you do buy curriculum, it usually comes in quarterlies, if you are writing or creating your own be sure and break your lessons into quarters (four thirteen week sessions), or into even smaller sessions (four to six weeks sessions). This helps keep the students attention; keeps the class moving forward; and creates natural breaks for new teachers to take over.

Help both your teachers and your students by rotating your teachers. The old thought of recruiting Sunday school teachers was to secure a teacher and have them teach for life, with no breaks or chances to opt out. Offering your teachers short teaching stints is much more attractive to them; it gives them a starting date and an ending date, and the opportunity to opt out. It also gives you the opportunity not to invite them back if need be.

I have my teachers teach for a maximum of thirteen weeks, and then rotate out. I also only allow them to teach for twenty-six weeks per year. When they are not teaching I make sure that they are attending an adult class.

I never allow my teachers to teach alone, but insist that there are two adult teachers in every class (preferably one male and one female).

There are huge benefits to working with your teachers to pair them with certain topics, and with certain age groups. Some adults will teach on any topic, and lead either junior high or senior high; while others are more specific about what topics and which age groups they will teach.

Regardless of who your teachers are, and how you rotate them, be sure and educate them, train them, resource them and encourage them. These four steps help them to become better teachers, improves the ministry and makes you look good as the one in charge.

Youth Group to Youth Ministry
to Youth Family

I strongly believe the most successful approach to youth ministry is one based upon a relational model. Many years ago I developed the idea of Youth Group to Youth Ministry to Youth Family.

Simply put, a youth group is any group of teenagers that hang out and do things together: sports team, scout troop, band, club . . . There does not have to be any spiritual significance to have a youth group. Sadly, there are churches all across America that have nothing more than a group of students who meet once a week, hang out, go on outings, and have no spiritual significance . . . they are just a youth group.

A youth ministry is a spiritually based group of students where ministry is happening, and teenagers are learning, growing and serving. However, this group of students must learn that church and youth ministry is not what they do, but who they are in order to reach the next level: youth family.

God did not create man to be alone, and He did not create humans to journey through life alone. A youth family is that church based spiritual group of students who do life together; not just on Sundays and Wednesdays, but every day . . . at church, at school, at work and at play.

In our ministry we constantly use words such as "brother" and "sister". We model and encourage uplifting language, as well as good, positive, appropriate touch and hugs between our adults and students, and between our students and students.

Taking a youth group to a youth ministry and then to a youth family creates a good, safe, inviting place for teenager to belong; but it also takes a continual effort, as the ebb and flow of youth ministry constantly changes the makeup of your students. Honestly, as hard as we strive, on occasion we still find ourselves more as a youth ministry and less of a youth family.

I once had a particular class of students that truly understood the concept of a youth family. They attended school together, played sports together, came to church and youth together and literally grew up together. For their senior prom, the boys from this amazing class decided to ask their sisters from church to be their dates. When asked about this decision, the boys shared that they wanted to make sure that their sisters all had the opportunity to attend prom, and that they wanted to make sure that they would be safe and have fun. This photo of my teenagers attending prom together is one of my most favorite photos in my nineteen years of ministry.

Youth Ministry Name

By naming your youth ministry you create a brand to promote and something for your students to associate with. Along with your name you can create a logo to help with the branding of your ministry.

Warning: Be creative. Do not regurgitate an already over used youth ministry name such as: U-Turn or 180 or Fusion (I apologize if this is the name of your ministry).

To create some ownership in the ministry host a contest and have the students contribute ministry names and logos. Offer a prize for the winner such as a gift certificate to the next youth outing, or steak dinner with their favorite adult volunteer.

Remember, students who name the ministry will own it; as will the students who are currently active when the name is given; so it is a good thing to think about renaming the ministry every seven or so years, because incoming seventh graders will have no connection to the name and brand.

At my current church I kept the old name but created a new logo shortly after arriving. Looking back I should have renamed the ministry within the first year, thus creating some distance between myself and the former youth pastor. Several years later we did rename the ministry from F.L.O.C. (Faithful Loving Outrageous Christians) to 501 Youth (based on Ephesians 5:1 – Follow God's example, therefore, as dearly loved children) (1).

T-Shirts

Everybody loves wearing a cool shirt, and what better way is there to promote your ministry then with t-shirts?

We print an annual t-shirt for our students and adult chaperones that attend our state youth convention in the fall. I budget for this shirt so that it is a free gift to them. We also print a shirt for our bi-annual trip to our international youth convention; again this is a gift for the students and adults who attend. Shirts do not have to be gifts, though; instead they can be designed, printed and sold.

I confess I am not an artist or a designer; I can barely draw stick figures. This is where I rely on the artists in my ministry. Sometimes I call on our resident artist, Maggie; other times I ask students to help; and still other times I simply host a design contest. I also confess that during my nineteen years I have had my share of bad t-shirts and designs; like the lime green soccer jerseys I had printed when my youth group was loaded with high school football players (we all know how much football players love soccer players, and then to ask them to wear a soccer jersey . . . What was I thinking?).

We take an annual snow skiing trip in January, however a shirt would be pointless on this trip, as it would be covered by our snow clothes. So one winter we partnered with a charity that knit us hats and sewed a label on them that read "My Hat Fed 50 Kids". We purchased fifty hats for $10 each and wore them while on the slopes. Several of my kids continue to wear these hats every ski trip.

Borrow, Tweak and Steal

One of the skills all youth leaders must acquire is the ability to borrow, tweak and steal from other youth leaders and ministries. As good as you are, and as good as your youth ministry is, there are always other leaders and ministries doing really good, cool and awesome stuff that you need to borrow, tweak and steal from in order to improve your own ministry.

I have personally borrowed, tweaked and stolen games, promotional methods, curriculum ideas, small group set ups, graphics, events, and names & themes.

I learned the game Diaper Dodge Ball from my long-time friend Doug. After attending a church while on sabbatical I decided to change the name of my summer Wednesday night Bible study from Back Yard Bible Study to Summer Nights. While on a college visit I was inspired by a girls dorm late night meeting that they called Sex & Chocolate; which I turned into a Sunday night, girls only, discussion on health, puberty, boys, dating and sex hosted by my female adult leaders, a health care professional, and a local school counselor. The chocolate came into play by building a chocolate buffet complete with a chocolate fountain. To counter balance that evening with my boys I hosted the same set up, only we served chicken on the grill and called it The Breast Sex Ever. (Not, really; we called it Man Up). And, every year, while at summer camp, I learn team building games that I use with both my students and my ministry team.

That is what this book is really about, me giving you permission to borrow, tweak and steal from me and my ministry.

Go To Events

Figure out your group's favorite go to events, and make sure that these appear on your calendar. For us those events are snow skiing, summer camp, amusement park, canoe trip, state youth convention, New Year's event, concerts, ten foot banana split . . .

Just remember, as your ministry ebb and flows every year and completely changes every six to seven years, the go to favorites of your group may, and will, change.

Regardless of the ebb and flow my ministry experiences, skiing, camp and convention remain go to events for us. However, there were years that we were taking van loads of kids to concerts four to six times a year, and the last concert I attended there were only three students with me.

When the ebb and flow takes the group in new directions, be flexible and go with it. This may mean tweaking old events to update them, or creating whole new events.

For several years our New Year's event was a mobile lock-in that started at the local YMCA and eventually ended back at the church. We then tweaked it from playing sports at the YMCA to watching a professional hockey game followed by a lock-in. When the local hockey team folded, it forced us to change the format again; however, we still do a New Year's event.

Meeting Places

This is where you can truly be creative. Just because you may have a youth room does not mean you always have to meet there. If you are leading a Bible study with a dvd curriculum, meet in the home of the church member with the largest flat screen and family room. Flag football should be played at the home of the church member with the largest backyard. Girl's only meetings should be hosted in a home that is warm, safe, comfortable and inviting. Bon fires need to be held down on the farm (and include a hay ride). Guy's only meetings should be held in the corner booth of the best wings place in town. Summer Bible studies have to be at the home of the person who has a swimming pool. Hot tubs are great during winter. Coffee shops are awesome for senior high and college age students. City parks with awesome play grounds and lots of green space are ideal for junior high students.

Even if you opt to use your youth room more times than not, change the way it looks. Re-arrange or change out the furniture, re-paint every two years, add lighting, get rid of old stuff, trade the ping pong table for air hockey, and always decorate to match the current holiday or the current theme of your study.

Stay For A Generation

Regardless if you are a full time, part time or volunteer youth leader, commit to stay at least one generation of students; which is six to seven years, depending on if sixth graders are a part of your ministry or not.

When I was in college I was taught that the average stay of a youth pastor, across denominational lines, was eighteen months; and I believed it. So when I hit eighteen months at my first ministry I was very proud. At the three year mark I thought I had accomplished something because I had stayed twice as long as the national average. As I worked my way towards five years, and then eight years, I began looking around and asking other youth pastors how long their tenures had been. What I discovered was that everyone I talked to was staying well over eighteen months, but not enough of them were staying for a generation.

Fourteen years into youth ministry, and half way through my master's degree, I had a professor share with me that he and some collogues had done a study and found that the national average was not eighteen months, but closer to three years; which is still only half of a generation of students.

I left my first ministry after eight and half years, and when I was in the interview process of the church I am currently serving, I entered into a covenant with the church leaders where I would not talk to, nor interview with, any other churches, and they agreed that they would not talk to, nor interview, any other candidates until God had revealed His will concerning our situation. After I was hired I prayed that God would protect me and my ministry by not allowing the temptation of another church or ministry to enter into my life. During my ten year tenure here I have only had one job offer; and it was easy to turn down. This is God's confirmation in my life and my ministry that this is where He wants me to be: serving the church and my students for more than a generation.

Best friends Megan and Molly had just entered the youth group as new seventh graders shortly before I arrived in Eaton. Together, we journeyed through their junior high and high school years. They were highly involved in my ministry and in the life of the church, and I, in turn, was highly involved in their lives. I cheered Molly on as she played soccer, basketball and softball, and Megan as she played volleyball; and watched them both on Friday nights as they were both in the marching band. The three of us shared many dinner tables together. I was a guest in both of their homes and they were always welcome in mine. I was in the bleachers the day they walked across the football field, and across the make shift stage of their high school graduation; an event I would not have celebrated with them had I not stayed for a generation. Four years later Rhonda and I traveled to the University of Toledo to see Molly graduate with her bachelor's, and a week later we were at Anderson University to watch Megan graduate with hers; again, events I would not have not attended had I not stayed longer than a generation.

Every June and Every Six Years

Every full time youth pastor has been asked (and more than once), "When are you going to get your own church?" or "When are you going to become a real pastor?"

The reality of those two asinine questions is that students are the church, and youth pastors work more hours and have a harder job than any other pastor on staff. Oh, yeah, I went there.

A senior pastor's congregation changes when babies are born, families join the church, families leave the church, and when people die. A youth leader's congregation changes every June when we graduate seniors and bring in our new sixth or seventh graders. And, every six to seven years we have a completely different congregation.

As we ride the ebb and flow of youth ministry and youth culture, and plan the direction of our ministry, we must keep these two inevitable facts in mind.

Deep Pockets

Once you have been serving in your church long enough to establish relationships with the adult population that has neither children nor grandchildren involved in the youth ministry, yet has a passion to support students and student ministries, partner with them to financially support your ministry and your students.

Public relations will go a long way in gaining financial support from these adults, such as, meeting them for lunch to share about the ministry, inviting them to your youth room, to a youth meeting or on an event so that they can see for themselves, and by sharing pictures, stories and personal testimonies with them.

I once invited a retired pastor to go to summer camp with us, as we were in need of a counselor. That one week that he spent with me and my students has him hooked as one of our biggest ministry supporters.

Do not ask for a blank check to throw a pizza party with, instead ask for a specific dollar amount to send kids to summer camp, or to buy a ministry tool, or to scholarship students on a missions trip.

Build Your Own Waffle Night

Borrow a bunch of waffle irons from your parents and church members (a bunch is defined by however many you need for the size of your group). Have each student bring an item: waffle mix, cooking spray, butter, syrup, chocolate chips, blueberries, peanut butter . . .

Mix up several bowls of batter, plug in the irons and let the students build their own waffles. Kick it up a notch and have an adult make eggs to order, and another fry bacon and sausage.

You can substitute waffles with tacos, coneys, baked potatoes, salad, French bread pizza, or whatever other food students can build their own for dinner.

These nights work great with a four to six week long small group; simply rotate the menu item each week.

Must Have Ministry Tools

Below is a list of must haves to pull off some of your ministry events. Collect these items via donations or garage sales and stock pile them in a hidden closet of your church so that other ministries do not walk away with them:

- Power strips / Surge bars
- Extension cords
- Camera
- Coffee Pots
- Coolers
- Hot Dog Sticks
- Water Bombs / Sponge Balls / Water Guns
- Football
- Flag Football Belts
- Frisbee
- Volleyball & Net
- Kickball & Bases
- Tennis Balls
- Cones
- Yard Games

Totes

As you plan events you will collect needed items to put them on. If you plan on making these annual events then you need to keep these items and store them away in clearly marked totes and have them well organized.

My totes hold the following events:

- Graduation banquet
- Red Hat Dinner
- Fair Parking T-Shirts
- Brown's Tree Auction
- Candy Easter Egg Supplies
- Sweetheart Dinner

Find a Need and Meet It

Jesus said in Mark 12:31, "The second is this: 'Love your neighbor as yourself.' There is no commandment greater than these." (2).

Early in my ministry one of my mentors explained Jesus' words as simply finding a need and meeting it.

Part of your ministry must be servant-hood. Jesus came as a servant. We are to imitate Jesus; therefore, we are to be servants; thus, we are to find needs and meet them.

Practicum would be teaching our students this and, more importantly, modeling before them how to live daily lives of finding and meeting needs. The fun part of this is the creativity that students can unleash on meeting the needs of those around them.

I live and serve in Ohio, which is obviously a land locked state. However, Hurricane Ike made it to Preble County. Trees were down, power was off, and schools were closed. On Monday and Tuesday my two sons and I spent the days going from church family to church family checking on them and cutting up trees and hauling away the wood and brush.

On Wednesday, instead of holding our regular youth meeting, we put out the word that we would be taking the church vans to Brother and Sister Bush's to cut up some fallen trees. This was before texting and Face Book, so we had to rely on e-mail and phone calls. I knew we would have fewer students than if we had just had youth group; surprisingly, we still had over twenty students and adults show up. We travelled to the Bush's house, served them a hot meal, cut and cleared the downed trees, ate fresh-from-the-oven brownies, and ended the evening by having students pray over this dearly loved elderly couple. Ike created the opportunity, and our students met the need.

Stay True to Your Denomination

If your denomination offers ministry events (summer camp, youth convention, sports rally, overnighter . . .) attend and support them. These events may be on a local, district, state, regional, or national level; regardless of what level they are offered on, attend and support them.

If these events are lacking and you feel that they are not worth attending, and that your students will not benefit from attending, then choose to become a part of the solution to improving the event, and building a better ministry opportunity.

If your denomination does not offer such events, choose carefully which non-denominational events you will attend. Here is my caution: these events come to town, do their ministry, and leave (maybe to return next year). The hazard is that they leave behind no support system for your attending students, or the decisions they may make.

The Church of God Reformation Movement in Ohio has done a good job of creating and sustaining events on the local, district and state levels. Some of these events include Stark County Roller Skating (which includes nine congregations and runs during the school year); North East Ohio Winter Retreat (which invites over sixty congregations); youth events during each of the five district camp meetings; seven weeks of summer camp at our state campgrounds; and the state youth convention (which hosts over fifty congregations and over 800 delegates).

The national office of the Church of God Reformation Movement also hosts their International Youth Convention every two years that is attended by over 5,000 delegates.

What Ohio Church of God youth leaders see happening with our students is that they grow up together at these events,

anticipate seeing one another at said events, create deep friend-
ships, end up attending college together, and some even marry one
another. Literally, our students are doing life together, as a very
large, extended youth family.

More importantly, our youth leaders are doing ministry together. We are building relationships with one another, and with
one another's students; thus creating an inner-woven ministry
support system for our students.

Attend Their Stuff

There is a powerful message sent to students when you show up to their stuff: sixth grade graduations, sporting events, musicals, band & choir concerts, scout promotions, National Honors Society inductions, award ceremonies . . .

It is important to let your student know that you will be attending. Arrive early enough to see them prior to the event. Hang out afterwards to hug, love and congratulate them; and do not forget to take pix with them.

Here in Eaton there is a football tradition (regardless if it is a home or an away game) that after the game, after the coach's speech, and after the seniors lead the team in their fight song, the parents and fans mob the field to hug, love and congratulate the boys. Every Friday night I go home drenched in sweat and smelling like I had played under the lights and all I did was hug players after the game.

Youth Pastor Heather Flies shares her story of a junior high wall flower that timidly invited her to come watch her twirl her flag in a color guard competition. Heather and her husband drove over an hour to the field to watch a five minute performance. But she arrived early enough to see her student prior to her performance, and stayed afterwards for pictures, hugs, love and congratulations. The story ends with the girl transforming from a wall flower to an active member of Heather's ministry.

I will be honest and tell you that some of the events you will attend will be painful to sit through, but very well worth it. I have sat through junior high band concerts and have heard Hot Cross Buns played way too many times; I have endured nineteen years of high school graduation speeches; been to countless National

Honors Society candle lighting ceremonies; watched endless sporting events; been to a variety of plays and musicals. . .

Yet, the message you send to both your students and their parents when you are in the stands or on the sidelines is that you truly love them, and that they are important to you. You also send a messages to other students and parents who are watching; messages about you, your ministry, your church, and most importantly, about the love of Christ.

Birthdays

Everyone loves to have their birthday remembered and recognized. A simple way to love and celebrate your student's birthdays is by honoring them with a card. In the digital world we live in it is easy to send an e-mail or to post on a student's Face Book page or to even send a tweet; but the lost art of sending a birthday card through the mail is the ministry punch of love that students prefer.

When the opportunity presents itself, take birthday celebrations even further. How many times has a student's big day landed on a Sunday or a Wednesday? When this happens provide cupcakes or ice cream in honor of that student.

Take advantage of when a student is with you on a youth outing, event or trip on their birthday and celebrate with them on the road.

One year at junior high camp my wife snuck into town and bought a cake and we had our students meet us in the pastor's cottage to celebrate Jordan's thirteenth birthday. We once honored two students who shared the same birthday with cupcakes during our ski trip. We have had countless birthday celebrations in hotel rooms across the country as students turned another year older while on youth outings, events and trips.

P.S.—Don't forget to celebrate the birthdays and anniversaries of the adults who minister alongside of you.

Breakfast on the Road

It is necessary that you feed your students breakfast while on the road. However, there are times when, due to group size and scheduling, it will be hard or impossible to go out to breakfast. Therefore, be creative (and cut costs) by supplying breakfast bags.

Depending on the size of your group and the length of your trip you can charge each delegate $2-5 to build a breakfast budget.

Collect the money from those who will be attending. Poll the students as to what breakfast items they prefer and write a shopping list, then go shopping. Divide the food into paper grocery bags. Give each room one bag with the instructions that this is their breakfast food for the entire trip, and that they need to ration it so that it lasts; warn them that if they eat it all on the first morning then they will go hungry the rest of the mornings.

Your grocery list should be made up of grab and go, hand held, breakfast foods such as fruit, breakfast bars, gummies, Pop Tarts, individually wrapped pastries, juice boxes . . .

I had been using this method of feeding my students for years, and it works. However I was bringing home a lot of leftover food, as some students do not eat breakfast. Finally, after years of packing food back home I decided to change my method. Instead of collecting money and assembling breakfast bags I simply added the line Breakfast Food to their "What To Bring" list. With this change I was able to cut $2-5 from the cost of the trip per delegate; students could make personal food choices, and could pack as much or as little as they wanted. Our initial use of this new method seemed to work, and we plan on using this method again for weekend outings, and short trips.

However, on a recent seven day, out of state trip, I did assemble hotel room bags. And, yes, we did pack a lot of left-over food on to the bus for the trip home; however, most of it was eaten during the two day ride back to Eaton.

What I have learned is that both methods work, and both have their pros and cons. Depending on the specifics of the trip will determine how I feed my students in the future.

Carry In Dinners

Every church in America hosts carry in dinners. You can use this same premise in youth ministry. Take advantage of small group settings, Sunday night gatherings, or summer Bible studies to train students on how carry in dinners work. Have each family provide a covered dish or dessert while the youth ministry provides the main dish and drinks.

It cuts your budget costs of providing meals, teaches students the importance of serving one another, and takes the responsibility of food off of you and your team members.

Here are the rules we play by: One covered dish or dessert per family, not per student. A bag of chips does not count as a covered dish. I remember one of my first attempts at this and we literally had burgers on the grill, cans of pop and fifteen bags of chips. If no one brings food, only meat and drinks will be served. If everyone brings dessert, only meat, drinks and sugar will be served. There will be nights that will be dessert heavy, but the students never seem to complain.

If you are serving up a specific meal, such as burgers on the grill, be sure to assign food items to students that are needed, or that complement the dish: buns, cheese, lettuce, tomatoes, onions, bacon . . .

Tacos: hard shells, soft shells, lettuce, tomatoes, cheese, sour cream, beans, picante sauce . . .

Waffles: butter, syrup, chocolate chips, blueberries, milk, orange juice, bacon, sausage . . .

Backyards

Backyards are great meeting places for both Bible studies and social gatherings. Create a list of families from your church that have awesome backyards and rotate using them.

During the summer months we totally change our Wednesday night youth service. During the school year we call it Open House, meet in our youth room at the church from 6:00-7:30 pm, and include game time, announcements, worship, prayer and a lesson. During the summer we move outdoors to various backyards; rename it Summer Nights, meet from 6:00-8:00 pm, have a carry in dinner, either swim in the host's pool or play yard games, give announcements and then have an in-depth Bible study.

Backyards are also great when hosting guy's only Bible studies. In the fall we host a four week guys only where we play flag football in the host's yard, then eat man-food (burgers, wings, chili dogs, chicken, pizza . . .) while going through our study.

In October, the backyard (or farm) that is large enough to host a bon fire (and hay ride) is the perfect place to be. Here in Eaton we also have access to yards that sit next to a creek; are big enough for wiffle ball games; have a pond; and are located next to a city park.

Play Games

Kids love to play; furthermore, kids need to play. Play games just for the fun of it; for the benefit of team building; and to teach and illustrate a point. Most importantly, make play a routine part of your ministry.

If your church has a gym, awesome! If your church has a large piece of green space, even better! Make it a point to utilize these often. We use our five acres of green space in the fall and spring, and move to our gym in the winter.

There are a ton of school yard classics that kids love to play: kick ball, wiffle ball, volley ball, knock-out, twenty-one, flag football. . . Let your group dictate their favorites; however, do not get stuck in a rut playing the same game or games every time you get together.

Some of my group's favorite games are: Scruples, Apples to Apples, Uno, Spoons—we use giant 8"x10" playing cards and large plastic cooking spoons, knock-out, flag football, diaper dodge ball, schizm, king of the ping pong table, upset fruit basket, hand squeeze relay, ninja tag, finger pull (of course, my junior high boys love to play pull my finger).

On occasion we will host a month long tournament pitting the students against the adults. Each Wednesday night we pick a game to play: ping pong, ninja tag, guitar hero, knock-out, ring-a-round-the-ping-pong-table, schizm, diaper dodge ball . . .

We keep a running score, with the winning team earning bragging rights and whatever I have placed up for grabs. Usually if the students lose they have to clean the youth room from top to bottom. If the adults lose one of men has to shave off their mustache and beard (which has yet to happen, but I do have a pretty clean youth room).

Continually resource yourself with game ideas from books, the internet, the game isle of your local store, your local gym teacher, your summer camp staff, other youth pastors . . . And watch the television show Minute To Win It. I truly believe that the creators of this show were once youth leaders, or got most of their ideas from us. The games on this show are easy to set up, inexpensive, and some of your students have seen the show and are convinced that they can win it.

Something I learned from the television show Whose Line Is It Anyway is that points are free, so give points out like Halloween candy. Students are more excited about earning 1000 points for their team over just getting five or ten points. I tell my students that they can spend their points at the points store later, where they can buy more points.

Diaper Dodge Ball

Buy the largest, cheapest box of disposable diapers that you can find. Unfold each diaper as if preparing to put it on a baby's butt. Fold each diaper as if it were a used, wet diaper. Be sure to use the adhesive tabs to tape the folded diapers. Wrap duct tape one time around each diaper. For around $10 you have just made yourself ninety diaper bombs that are reusable for years.

Regardless of how hard one throws a diaper bomb, players will feel the bombs when hit with it, but the soft diapers do not hurt. To help ensure no collateral damage we instilled the six foot rule that states a player must be 6' away or further when throwing a diaper bomb.

We play different versions of diaper dodge ball to keep the students interested: boys vs girls; students vs adults; junior high vs senior high; with boundaries; without boundaries; shrinking field, with barricades to hide behind; open field; two teams; four teams; every person for themselves . . .

We recently invited our fifth and sixth graders to join us for a game as a way of introducing them to our ministry, our students and our adults.

Schizm

Schizm is a volleyball-like game of elimination that my students and I learned years ago at summer camp. One of the college camp teams brought it with them, and through the years I have seen more and more groups learning to play.

Schizm can be played either indoor or outdoor on a volleyball court.

Divide your group (adults included) into two equal teams.

Give each team a volleyball.

Count down "Three-two-one schizm".

At this point the players with the balls throw them over the net. Opposing players must catch the balls and throw them back over the net.

If the ball is thrown and fails to make it over the net, the thrower is out of the game. However, if a teammate catches the ball before it hits the ground, the thrower is still in the game.

If a ball is thrown over the net and is not caught and hits the ground, the player closest to the ball when it hits the ground is out of the game.

If a player attempts to catch a ball, but fails to do so, yet has touched the ball, and the ball hits the ground that player is out of the game. However, if after the first player fails to catch the ball, a teammate successfully catches the ball prior to it hitting the ground, no player is out of the game.

If more than one player touches the ball, but none of them catch the ball, and the ball hits the ground, the first player to touch the ball is out of the game.

If a player throws a ball and it lands out of bounds, that player is out of the game.

If a player hits a thrown ball with their ball, both balls become dead balls and no player is out. However, if a player throws their ball at another ball and misses, and their ball does not make it over the net, that player is out of the game; and if the opponent's ball hits the ground the player standing closest to the thrown ball is also out of the game.

If a player hits a thrown ball with their ball and the thrown ball is caught by them or a teammate this is called a schizm. Their ball, because it hit another ball, is a dead ball and can hit the ground. The opponent's ball that was hit and then caught allows a player who is out of the game to return to the game.

If in the above scenario both balls are caught prior to hitting the ground two players who are out of the game are allowed back in, as this is called a double schism.

If a player is holding a ball and catches a thrown ball, this, too, is a schizm and a player who is out of the game is allowed back in.

If a player catches a thrown ball, and is the first player to catch the next thrown ball, while still holding the first ball, this is also a double schizm and two players who are out of the game are allowed back in.

Once one team has been eliminated the game is over.

Other rules:

1. Balls must be caught before being thrown; no volleyball hits.

2. No throw downs, spikes, or hard throws; balls must be catchable.

3. No bouncing or dribbling of balls.

4. No player may have more than one ball in their hands at a time; unless they are catching them, or are the final player for their team.

5. When players are eliminated they need to stand in a line in the order that they were eliminated so that when a schizm occurs they can re-enter the game in that same order that they were eliminated.

There are a variety of other rules, and I have found that every group plays a little differently. The following are rules you can tweak and change to keep the game fresh:

1. Whether a player can or cannot move if they have a ball in their hand (the final player can move with a ball in their hand).

2. Speed schizm—as soon as the ball is caught it must be thrown.

3. Out of play—play is suspended if a ball has been thrown out of bounds.

4. Playing with three or four balls.

5. How you divide your teams: junior high vs senior high; adults vs students; girls vs boys; by school district; have captains choose . . .

When we pit girls vs boys we add rules such as boys can only catch with one hand, and must throw with their opposite hand; we allow the girls to steal two to three boys to be on their team; and give each girl two lives.

Order of Importance

The reality of youth ministry is that you only have six to seven years with your students, and there is a lifetime of important things that need to happen, and need to be taught. The question becomes, what will you do and teach, and what will you not do and not teach.

As you plan out what you will and will not do there are a variety of variables that you have to factor in: schedules, finances, value, and timing.

When scheduling your youth ministry calendar you need to take into consideration the schedules of the students, the church, the event, and your personal, private time. For some youth ministry's Friday nights in the fall are horrible times for events as too many students are involved in football, marching band, cheerleading and management and training. However, the weeks between sports during the winter and spring provide great opportunities.

I once planned a trip for my adults to attend a game of the local minor league baseball team. I ordered and paid for tickets in March; but I had failed to look at our church calendar, which had our all church picnic planned for the same date. It worked out for me and my team, but it was a long day.

The same is true when you consider finances; you must be aware of the financial resources of your students and their families, the church's, your youth ministry budget, and your own personal monies. You do not want to invest time and energy into an event only to have no one able to afford to attend. I have made many decisions based on the financial costs of the event. Here in Preble County we have two middle schools that send their eighth grade classes on an annual trip to Washington D.C. at the estimated cost of $800 per student. I have to remember my eighth grade students whose parents are paying this $800, and paying $150 for state youth convention, $200 for church summer camp, and whatever else we decide to do throughout the school year and summer. Available finances, or lack of, force us, as youth pastors, to become frugally creative.

If an event does fit into your schedule, and the cost is manageable, the next concern becomes the value of the event. What is the benefit to the students and to the ministry by participating, and is it worth the time, money, effort and energy. For me, and my students, summer camp and state youth convention are nonnegotiable. These two events are too valuable in the spiritual molding of my teenagers lives to not attend. Therefore, we communicate with our parents the dates and costs of both of these events as far out as we possibly can. On the other hand, we have supported and participated in an annual student leaders training weekend since its inception. Recently, due to the deterioration of this event, we have had to re-evaluate the value of this weekend for our student leaders. At the time of this writing our decision is to go one more year, so that we can graduate our two students who will complete the program this year, but we will not begin any new students into the program. After this year's weekend we will make a final decision as to the future of our participation.

When planning your calendar you need to remember that your students have families, school, sports, band / choir, church, work and friends competing for their time. Maybe, instead of adding one more thing to their already over packed calendars, we create fewer events that are more impactful with greater spiritual value.

Every year my ministry participates in the following annual events: ski trip, summer camp, state convention, and every two years we attended our international youth convention. All other events, trips and outings are negotiable, which means they may or may not appear on the calendar. When a new event does pop up we sometimes have to work really hard in order to get it on to our calendar; sometimes it makes it on to the calendar, and sometime it does not.

There is an annual Christian concert in the neighboring county that happens to fall on the same night of our church's annual business meeting, therefore, we never attend. Last year the date of the concert moved back one week and we immediately put it on our calendar, and took over twenty people, and have made plans to return again this year.

There was a national girl's only event that came to our area one year; the dates of the event happened to overlap with a student leaders conference that we send certain students to. The compromise was that we would do both, but the student leaders had to attend their conference and not the girls only event. Though the girl's only went over well with our students, and had great spiritual value, it has yet to return to our area, so we have only attended one time.

Because summer is such a busy time for our students and their families, we either go to the local amusement park or canoeing, but we never do both in the same summer.

Many times we have put effort into an event or activity only to cancel due to scheduling conflicts; most recently my wife headed up a girls only half-nighter. She and another lady planned it out, promoted it very well, and on the Wednesday prior to the event had to cancel due to the fact that only one girl would be able to attend due to student's schedules.

We live three hours south of the number one amusement park on the planet, Cedar Point (at one time it claimed seven of the top ten roller coasters in America). I have often considered taking a trip there with my students, but the deciding factor is finances and value. The last time that I, personally, was there I only rode seven rides, and I was there from the time the gate opened to the time the gate closed. I cannot justify the expense for the experience. So instead we travel forty-five minutes to a smaller park, which costs less, is closer, and allows the students and adults to ride more rides.

Teachers

You must take care of your teachers, whether they lead Sunday school, Wednesday Night, or Small Groups. Below are some simple ways that you can care for them, and ensure their longevity in your ministry.

Rotate your teachers on a regular basis. My Sunday school teachers lead for one quarter (thirteen weeks) at a time and then rotate out. They are also only allowed to teach a total of two quarters (twenty-six weeks) a year. If their personal schedules do not allow them to teach for thirteen weeks at a time, be flexible and work with them. There is a man in our church who taught a three week stint in senior high Sunday school. He did a wonderful job, the students loved having him, and he really enjoyed it. For years we have been trying to get him back into the classroom, however his schedule did not permit it. Finally, I was able to pin him down to lead a four week study with our senior high. I needed to be flexible and patient in order to get him, and he was worth it.

Match your teachers to the topics that they are comfortable leading or are an expert in. Some of our students wanted a lesson on the topic of tongues. Instead of me teaching this lesson, I recruited our Senior Pastor to join us for Wednesday Night Open House and to lead the discussion (our students loved it). For our One Night Only Girls Only I recruited a female nurse and a female school counselor to lead the discussion. That same night we hosted a One Night Only Guys Only which was led by a male doctor and a male health care professional.

Depending on what the subject matter is, be willing to bring in special guest teachers for certain topics, whether the topics take one session, or four, six or eight weeks. Having a fresh face and an expert on the subject is well worth the effort, and gives your regular teachers a break. We invited our worship pastor to be a part of, and or lead, when we host a Night of Worship; and a few years back he taught a four week series on worship.

Allow your teachers to use their gifts, skills and abilities, and encourage them to be creative. When my teachers have an idea for a lesson, series or a teaching method, it is rare that I say "no"; instead I encourage them and try my best to resource them to pull it off. I must brag, I have some truly creative adults on my team.

Even when you are surrounded with creative teachers and leaders, you still need to train them. Teach them how to write or choose curriculum. Work with them on different ways to tell, teach, and convey the story or lesson. Equip them with books of ideas that will help make them better communicators. And, if your budget will afford it, take them to youth ministry training seminars and conferences. My youth ministry assistant, Emily, and I attend a one day conference each fall where we sit under a nationally known youth leader / speaker. I had the opportunity to take one of my adults, Danny, with me to the National Youth Workers Conference. I have resourced my adults with books, magazine articles, videos, and blogs. All of which pay off huge dividends within my ministry.

Budget

I truly hope and pray that your church gives you a youth ministry budget. Sadly, I know many youth pastors who either have no budget or a very small budget; and when I mean small I am thinking about a certain church of 150 people, with a youth group of fifteen students, and a youth ministry budget of $500 annually. I know that some churches struggle financially, but I honestly feel that the dollar amount in the youth ministry line item of a church's budget speaks volumes as to the value that church puts on youth ministry.

When you propose your budget to your church leaders, do so with line items so that it is easy to explain to anyone who asks, and easy to keep in order, every ministry dollar you are asking for, given and spending.

Here are a few line items that may or may not need to be in your budget:

- Curriculum—this will cover curriculum for all of your youth meetings; however, try not to have this line item in your budget, but instead, try to have the Board of Christian Education pay for it out of their budget

- Event Scholarships—for students who need financial help in order to attend events such as summer camp or convention

- Adults—ask for funds to pay for as much as you can for your adult sponsors who will attending events, outings and trips

- Parking—most places you will go will charge you to park; either budget for this, or add it to the students cost for the event

- Fundraisers—because we all know you have to spend money to make money

- Food—this helps when you cover the main dish and drinks at youth gatherings

- Media—to cover both needed hardware and software

- Tools—see my chapter on ministry tools

- Special events—regardless of what the event is, ski trip, concerts, kick-off, finale, service projects, they all come with a price tag

- Give-a-Ways—because someone has to pay for all the cool stuff you give away during the year

Graduation Banquet

Honor your high school graduates with a banquet, regardless if the class is sixteen or one. Send an invitation to all of the graduates and their families; you can also open it to church members if you like. Provide a brag table for each graduate that they can decorate prior to the banquet. Set up a head table for the graduates. Have their parents serve them throughout the meal. Either have the students write a letter to their parents, or the parents write a letter to their students (we rotate every other year), and give them the opportunity to read them aloud during the evening.

As the youth leader prepare and give a sermonette directed to the graduates. Put together a power point slide show highlighting what the graduates have done during their six to seven years in youth ministry. End the evening by having the families surround their students and by the laying of hands. Invite the rest of the guests to surround the families. Then offer up a prayer for the graduates.

Hold the students for one finale group photo before they head their separate ways into college, career, or marriage . . . (these are some of my most cherished ministry photos).

This evening and the meal can be simple or exquisite. We serve chicken on the grill to our guests and steak on the grill to our graduates. We limit the invited guests to immediate family members of the graduates, and church staff.

Overnighters vs Half-Nighters

When I was younger and just beginning youth ministry I hosted overnighters three or four times a year. Looking back, these were poorly planned, poorly chaperoned and poorly executed events. Now that I am a lot older, and a bit wiser, I rarely host overnighters, and opt for the easier to pull off, yet rarely used, half-nighter.

The reasons are simple. Overnighters are exhausting, half-nighters not so much. Overnighters take a ton of adult chaperones, half-nighters not so much. Overnighters can be as long as ten hours, half-nighters are usually half as long. Overnighters have more risks and safety issues, half-nighters not so much.

Regardless of which one you are hosting, here are some things I have learned over the years:

If it is going to be an overnighter divide by age or by gender, or by both. Division helps with control and safety issues; it also lowers the number of students you will be dealing with for ten hours. If you do keep all of your students together, you will need to overload the number of adult chaperones you have, and provided gender specific areas for privacy and sleeping.

During overnighters it is a good idea to rotate your adults throughout the night. Have a team begin the event, another team relieve them part way through, and third team finish out the event.

Make sure that your allotted time is filled, and that there is little "free time" where students can be tempted to get themselves in to trouble.

One of the ways to keep overnighters and half-nighters moving is to literally be on the move; who says either one needs to be restricted to the church. Incorporate off-site places such as a roller rink, bowling alley, movie theater, ice cream place, sporting event, laser tag, progressive dinner . . . If you are restricted to the church bring in items such as laser tag, tag ball, diaper dodge ball, karaoke . . .

A great way to end an overnighter is to have adults come to the church and cook breakfast for the students: pancakes, bacon, eggs, milk, orange juice . . .

Some of my past overnighters and half-nighters have looked like this: meet at the church; go roller skating / bowling / drive in movie; late night ice cream; group games; Karaoke; hide-n-seek / sardines; breakfast

Overnighters are great ways to connect with sister churches. While at my first church my group participated annually in a county-wide sports overnighter that was held at a local YMCA. After moving to my second church we began hosting a similar district-wide sports overnighter. Though they were promoted as sports overnighters, and were held in YMCAs, we offered events for the non-athletic students such as video games, swimming pool, and ping pong.

Candles & Air Fresheners

Most youth rooms simply do not smell pretty. It is because we deal with students . . . which include junior high boys. Scented candles and air fresheners should be on hand at all times, and commonly used in all of your meeting spaces.

Beyond covering up the smells and odors that come with working with students, candles and air fresheners help set and control the mood of the group (which works wonders when preparing for worship). Ask a local expert which scents and aromas will help set the mood you are looking for.

I once filled an entire 15,000 square foot ball room with a certain scent on a Sunday morning to help set the mood for a time of intimate worship that we had planned with 800 students. The area smelled really good, the students noticed the aroma, and worship was awesome that morning; not because of the scent in the air, but I believe it did play a part.

Budget vs Fundraisers

Keep these two items separate. Even though they are both monies set aside for youth ministry, it is wise to keep them separate. If you combine the two you will find certain church leaders who will look at your budget and think that you have enough, or even too much money, and will want to cut your church budget.

Do your best to spend your entire church budget before using your fundraising money. One of the reasons for this is if you annually have funds left over in your church budget leaders may cut your budget.

Another reason to keep them separate is that most funds from a church budget do not roll over at the end of a fiscal year, whereas money earned from fundraising does.

In order to keep our funds separate we actually use two different accounts and two different treasurers. The church treasurer tends to the funds given through the yearly church budget, and one of the adults from my ministry team tends to the funds earned through our fundraising.

It is a good accountability practice that protects all parties involved to have a volunteer, and not you, as the youth leader, act as your treasurer who will then work with you in controlling your fundraising monies.

Coffee & Hot Chocolate

Spend some money and purchase however many twelve cup coffee makers you need for the size of your group (my group needs three). Since my church already has a coffee bar, we use all three of our makers just to heat water, although, you may want to dedicate one for coffee if needed.

In our youth room we have provided our students with single serving coffee packets, tea bags and hot chocolate mixes on Sunday mornings and Wednesday nights during the late fall and winter.

We ask different parents to donate homemade cookies or muffins from time to time to compliment the coffee, tea and hot chocolate.

Roxy's Hot Chocolate Mix

- 25.6oz Powdered Milk
- 1# Nestle Instant Chocolate Drink Mix w/ Marshmallows
- ½# Coffee Mate
- 2c Powdered Sugar
- Mix all ingredients in a large container
- Mix 2 teaspoons in 8oz of hot water

Elementary Age Students

Youth ministry is geared towards junior and senior high students, but if you wait until students are in your youth ministry to build relationships with them then you have already lost precious time.

Visit the nursery and get to know which babies belong to which parents. Volunteer on occasion in the children's ministry (Sunday school, Vacation Bible School, Kids Church . . .) in order to get to know the younger students, and to begin relationships with them. My wife, Rhonda, and I have volunteered in the nursery, work with Vacation Bible School, and substitute teach the fifth and sixth grade Sunday school class.

Find ways to incorporate the fifth and sixth graders into your youth ministry throughout the year. As mentioned in another chapter, we invited the fifth and sixth graders to join us for diaper dodge ball. One fall we brought home a stack of t-shirts from our annual state youth convention and gave them to the sixth graders as we shared about convention, and then told them that they would be joining us next year for convention. I later found out that several girls who attended the same school all wore their new shirts the next day.

If your students have younger siblings, get to know them in anticipation to them joining the youth ministry.

Newsletter

As in any relationship, communication is vital. Develop a newsletter that you can use either monthly or bi-monthly. Your newsletter needs to be flexible enough that the info can be presented in print and mailed out to your students; in a mass e-mail; posted on your Face Book page; in a mass text message; or in a tweet.

If your church has a website, ask for a page that can be dedicated to youth ministry. If funding is not an issue, and your ministry is large enough to warrant one, you may want to host your own youth ministry website. If not, a great free alternative is to build and host a youth ministry Face Book page. You can find us on Face Book at: 501 Youth

One of the rules for each and every way that you choose to communicate is that these tools must be reserved for youth ministry news and information only. These are all great ways to communicate events, dates, times, addresses, changes in plans, websites, and event pictures; however, if you begin adding personal items, non-ministry news, forwards, and spam you will quickly lose your audience.

It is also important to keep up with the changes in media, and which ways your students are choosing to communicate; if none of them tweet, do not waste your time and energy.

Local Events

When looking for events to attend either as volunteers or as participants, look locally. What does your neighborhood, town, city, and county offer? Do they host an annual fair or festival? In Eaton we have the County Fair and the Pork Festival. Our ministry directs traffic during the fair as a fund raiser.

What parades come through your town? And are your students in these parades? Again, in Eaton, we have the parades that open the County Fair and the Pork Festival as well as the Memorial Day Parade, which a large number of my students participate in.

Does your town or city have a local theater or playhouse? Eaton does not, but several county schools put on plays and musicals, and two neighboring towns have small theaters. I have several students who perform on stage in these productions, and at these community theaters. Which make great, inexpensive youth outings, and create amazing opportunities for students to support one another. We regularly take groups of students to watch their brothers and sisters perform on stage.

Obviously, larger cities have more to offer, so for those who live in big cities you should look both locally in your church neighborhood, as well as what is happening on the other side of your city.

Dinner

Meals are vital to ministry. Jesus used the dinner table many times during his ministry. There are two things that happen at every dinner table: you eat, and you talk with those whom you are sharing the meal with.

Whether the meal is breakfast, lunch, dinner, or the fourth meal, and no matter if it is in a home or at a restaurant, the important part is that you are spending time with either a student or one of your team members.

One-on-One meal times are awesome because you dedicate all of your time and attention to that one student or adult. It is vital that one-on-one meals must be with the same gender student or adult. If you want to spend time with a student of the opposite gender, take your spouse along, or another adult volunteer. For me, I send either my wife or ministry assistant to dinner with my female students and adult leaders.

Group meal times are also just as awesome because the group sitting at the table has the opportunity to build relationships with one another and to invest in each other. We use group meal times when we are on the road; girl and guy only events; junior high and senior high only times . . .

Celebrating the accomplishment of a student over a meal is also vital to the relationship between adult and student. See my chapter on hosting a graduation banquet.

One year I received an unexpected, and large, monetary gift earmarked for youth ministry. I set aside a portion of that money to be used by my adult sponsors to take students out for a coke, ice cream or a meal. This was one of the best financial investments I have made during my nineteen years ministry career.

As you implement the use of meals in your ministry the students will find their favorites, and the group will develop their own food traditions. I take a group of student leaders on an annual three day training weekend, and it is our tradition to eat wings and then go for late night ice cream. I take a crew to our state youth convention early to help set up, and it is our tradition to eat at a local hole-in-the-wall for lunch. On Saturday of that same convention my group goes to dinner at their favorite BBQ place. Knowing that my son, Justin, and I are outdoorsman, the students will request wild game be served at carry-ins, and that the taco meat for our annual ski trip be made of venison.

Pictures

When I first entered youth ministry I used my background in photography to capture my students at different ministry events. I would print off two copies of every picture and use one as a promotional piece on the board outside my office; the other photo I would mail as a post card to the student whose face I could see in the picture. It was always awesome to see these picture post cards on the fridges of my students.

As technology changed so has my use of photos. I now pack and use my digital 35mm; I also recruit students to take pictures with their phones. During some events I ask certain students to be the official photographer and let them use my 35mm to capture the event. These pictures are used on our Face Book page and web site, in our newsletters, on our promotional posters, and in power point slide shows (especially the one we assemble for our graduation banquet).

Youth ministry photos that are easily seen on-line are great for personal relations between the youth ministry and parents, grand-parents, church people and leaders, as well as those who are looking for a church.

During the weeks of summer camp I carry my camera with me at all times. Each evening I add photo albums of the day's events to our Face Book page. I have found that my parents back in Eaton love seeing that their kids are okay, having fun, eating well, and making friends.

I encourage students and parents to copy our ministry pictures and use them on their own Face Book pages, and to print them off for their own use.

Couch and Ping Pong Table

I once picked up a very large, rounded love seat that was white in color, yet had a raised paisley design. We supplied the students with fabric markers and allowed them to color in the paisleys, thus making the couch very personalized, and very much their own. It took them a full school year of Wednesday nights to complete their artwork.

While out garage saleing one summer I found a very nice, hardly sat on white couch. I immediately knew what I would do with this couch. At our fall kick off that year I had the couch outside on our gravel parking lot where some of my adults were helping kids personalize the couch. I had a pile of latex gloves of various sizes and spray bottles of fabric dye. The students put on a glove, placed their hand on the couch, spread their fingers, and an adult sprayed various colors over the hands of the students, thus creating a burst of color with their white hand in the middle.

Several years later I built a ping pong table and painted it bright yellow. One Wednesday night I had the students paint the palms of their hands and press them on to the top of the table. Afterwards they signed their names in permanent marker next to their handprint.

There are many ways to personalize your meeting space, or the items in your meeting space. Just remember to keep up with your current students. Several years after we hand printed the ping pong table we re-painted the entire table and covered up the hands. The couch was so long ago that every student whose hand is on the couch has since graduated and moved on, yet the couch remains (mostly because it is cool, and because we need the butt-space), however my younger students want their own white couch to do the same with (which I am currently looking for).

Youth Room Furniture

If you have a dedicated space then you will need to furnish it. The cheapest way is with donated furniture; ask church families to remember the youth ministry when buying new furniture by donating their older pieces to you. Other places to find furniture is at garage sales, auctions, estate sales, and on-line.

A great place to find furniture is within the church itself. Take a walk through the church, look in every nook and cranny, if you find a piece of furniture that is not being used, or has not been claimed, steal it.

There are a few rules of thumb when accepting donated furniture. Make sure that the piece is coming from a non-pet and non-smoker home. Too many of your students may be allergic to pets and smoke, and it is not worth the risk of their discomfort. Do not accept easy chairs or recliners, as they take up too much real estate for one butt space. Do not accept sleeper sofas either; besides the obvious, they are too heavy to be moving around.

Understand that all of your furniture will have a short life expectancy, due to the use and abuse it will take on Sundays and Wednesday nights. One of my former students holds our church record for most pieces of furniture destroyed by one person. Lucas the Worm broke three stackable chairs, one love seat, and one couch.

As your group changes, your needs furniture needs will also change, therefore, collect a variety of pieces: couches, love seats, moon chairs, bean bags, high top tables & chairs, table & chairs . . . As your Sunday and Wednesday programs change, be willing to arrange and re-arrange your room. Not only does this help meet the needs you have, it also brings freshness to the look and feel of the room.

Desserts

Most of your students are in some stage of puberty . . . just beginning, deep in the middle, or towards the end. Regardless of what stage they are in, your students are hungry! It is important to feed them, and you can do so with very little financial investment.

Bottled water is cheaper than cans of pop. Two liters are also cheaper than cans. Buy beverages when they are on sale and stock pile them.

Stockpile candy that is on clearance after holidays . . . Halloween, Christmas, Easter, and Valentine's Day.

Get your parents on a rotation so that you can provide desserts during your meetings. Remind your parents that homemade is always better than store bought. Be sure to request desserts that are finger foods. By doing so you eliminate the need for paper products and students cannot pile a plate full to where other students go without.

Fun Food

Invest in a piece of ten foot pvc rain gutter. While you are playing a game or giving a lesson, have your adults line the gutter with aluminum foil and then build a ten foot Banana Split. Be aware that the assembly will take three to four adults ten to fifteen minutes. I recommend that some sections have all of the toppings, while other sections do not, as this helps to satisfy your picky eaters. After the students have taken pix with the split, give them each a bowl and spoon and let them devour the melting goodness by scooping as much as they want into their bowls.

The first time we built a ten foot Banana Split we handed each student a spoon and allowed them to eat straight from the gutter. However, we quickly learned that the gutter was on a slight incline which meant that it was all rolling downhill. Junior high boys were shoveling ice cream into their mouths as fast as they could, with most of it falling back out and into the gutter, thus rolling downhill towards the girls; who grossed out, set down their spoons and walked away.

Here is what you need to build your split: Neapolitan ice cream, bananas, chocolate syrup, strawberry topping, pineapple topping, cool whip, bowls, spoons (serving and eating), and napkins.

You can also use the gutter to build a ten foot Chili Dog (which is great for guys only events): loaves of bread, hot dogs, chili (with and without beans), plates, and forks.

Instead of feeding them the boring and over-used pizza, cook them dinner on the grill. Hot dogs are a youth ministry staple, but branch out and grill brats, sausages, burgers, and chicken; if you have a hunter in your church, as for a donation of venison steaks.

Although chicken breasts are bigger, thighs are cheaper and are a dark meat (which most students prefer). If you do grill breasts, consider cutting them in half to make them go further.

When you do fall back and order pizza, have it cut into squares in order for it to go further. I am not sure why, but squares seem to go further than slices.

If you are an outdoorsman, or if you have one in your church (which I know you do), treat your students to a wild game dinner (have burgers and dogs for those who are not feeling adventurous).

My youngest son, Justin, and I hosted a wild game dinner for my students where we served fish, squirrel, rabbit, duck and deer; we had burgers for the non-adventurous eaters. We encouraged the students to try a dish, most did, and most of those enjoyed what they ate. Most recently I grilled dove breasts wrapped in bacon with pineapple ka-bobs. I had twenty, and my students ate them all.

Though it is expensive, on occasion it is good to spoil your students with wing night. Depending on the size of your group will determine how you need to cook your wings: oven, slow cooker, or turkey fryer. Prepare them naked and provide a variety of sauces and sandwich baggies so that each student can customize their wings.

Appetizer night is a favorite of teenagers: chicken nuggets, taquitos, pigs-in-a-blanket, shrimp ring, pizza croissants, chips & dip, meatballs, little wienies . . .

Build Your Own _____ Night: taco, salad, waffle, French bread pizza, smoothies, baked potato . . .

One of my personal favorite fun foods is to fill a container full of candy and have the students guess how many pieces are in the container, and then give the container to the student whose guess is closest.

At the request of my children's director I built a sucker tree for one of her events. The tree stands 6' tall, looks like a real tree, and holds 100 Dum Dums; it resides in my youth room when not being used by the children's ministry. I keep it supplied with the Dum Dums that I buy on clearance the day after Halloween.

Summer Camp

Summer camp is a passionate subject for me. I grew up a ½ hour from my summer camp, which means I was there each summer as a camper. My youth group used the camp grounds for various events. I fished the lakes at the camp with my dad (and with my then high school girl friend, now wife, Rhonda). My mom even served on the kitchen staff one summer and my siblings and I lived in a camper on the grounds that summer, with my older brother and I having free reign of the camp: swimming, fishing, attending activities, fishing, staying up late, fishing, camp site hopping to mooch s'mores, and skipping evening chapel to go fishing.

Summer camp is a vital part of youth ministry, and I simply cannot stress enough the importance of getting your students to camp every summer. If your denomination offers a summer camping program I strongly suggest that you check into that program first. If it is a quality camp, I urge you to support and attend that camp.

You driving your students to camp is also vital. Youth ministry magic happens during long car rides when students are packed into the church van for hours with nothing to do but look out the window and carry on conversations with one another (a.k.a. – investing in one another through relational ministry). Sadly, I know too many youth ministries who leave it up to the parents to get their own students to and from camp, which is a lost opportunity for students to bond with one another.

I strongly urge you to spend the week with your students as their cabin counselor. If given the opportunity be the camp pastor; if not, be a camp teacher, or volunteer to serve on their planning team. I have been attending our summer camp for eighteen summers; most years I attend both junior and senior high. Over the years I have been a cabin counselor, camp pastor, morning teacher, dish washer, high ropes team member, flag football referee, grocery shopper, night security, "ambulance" driver, and all around gopher. Regardless of the role I play, it is important that I am on the grounds with the students.

Make attending summer camp an annual event; regardless of what other events you put on your summer calendar, take your kids to camp. Even though you are a youth leader, start your campers as young as you can. Our state camping program in Ohio begins with a Family Camp where parents attend with their grade K kids for a weekend. Every summer for the past ten years I have been sending campers from grade K through grade twelve. Prior to that, my previous church mostly sent junior and senior high students.

Either in the spring before camp opens or in the fall when camp closes take a group of campers to camp for a work weekend. Let them do the work that needs to happen to either open or close the camp. By doing so the camp gets needed help, and the students invest in, connect to, and form an ownership with the camp. They also begin and strengthen relationships with the camp director and staff members.

Summer camp is not a vacation. If your pastor, board chairman, deacons, elders, lay leaders or parents feel, think or believe that you going to summer camp with your students is a week of vacation, first have them contact me, second have them go to camp with you next summer as a cabin counselor.

On the flip side, I know a youth minister who would drive his students to camp every summer, but never stay. I asked him why he was not serving at camp as a counselor, a teacher, or a pastor and he replied that in order to do so he would have to use one of his personal weeks of vacation, per his senior pastor. This is wrong. Sadly, this is the attitude of many churches. Summer camp is one of the most vital aspects of youth ministry, and must be supported by you, your pastor, your church leaders, your congregation, your students and their parents. That particular youth minister left that church after just two years, and that church stopped coming to camp shortly after.

Sunday Nights

Most churches have done away with traditional Sunday night services; and most youth ministries meet on Sunday mornings for Sunday school, and on Wednesday nights for youth group. Instead of leaving Sunday night empty, utilized Sunday nights. We do so in two different ways.

First we offer short Bible Studies known as "Intense". These Intense studies last four to six weeks, and focus on a particular book, character, or topic from the Bible, or as a book study. We offer Intense studies as "guys only" and "girls only", or divide our students by junior high and senior high; we rarely offer them as a whole group, as part of the formula for success is to create small groups.

Intense groups meet in host homes, usually from 6:00-8:00 pm. The students arrive at 6:00 pm, each with a dessert or side dish and their Bible or book. The youth ministry provides the main dish, drinks and paper products. For the first hour we practice the art of the long supper. Then from 7:00-8:00 pm we intensely do our study.

The reason we call our Sunday Nights "Intense" is because we were not targeting every student, but those who were serious about growing in their relationship with Christ. If we are averaging forty-five students on Wednesday nights, we will average twenty on Sunday nights.

In-between our Intense offerings we host Super Sunday events. These are one & done extracurricular outings such as: bowling (combined with pizza), skating (roller or ice), dinner & dessert, movie (theater, drive-in or home), cook out & swim party, hiking, corn maze, pro sports event, paintball, flag football . . .

Super Sunday events are done solely for relational ministry purposes. These events help in building and maintaining a youth family.

Wednesday Night

It is important for you to give your Wednesday night youth meeting a cool name. We call ours "Open House"; which implies that the church is open for more than just youth group, and that it is a friend-friendly atmosphere.

Our "typical" Wednesday night schedule is:

5:30 PM	All church dinner
6:00 PM	Gathering time w/ music videos ping pong, air hockey, and video games
6:15 PM	Group game
6:30 PM	Announcements & Worship
7:00 PM	Lesson
7:30 PM	Hang time in the youth room and gym
8:00 PM	Go home

I say typical because I tell our students that they never know what was going to happen on Wednesday nights. One of the biggest challenges of a Wednesday night program is to keep it fun, and fresh; which is why the above sentence was written.

During our gathering time we offer drinks on a weekly basis: bottled water, cans of pop, hot water for cocoa and coffee, and whatever else we come up to serve. Although, thanks to a former student, Amy, who never drank pop, and would get on to me if there was no water in the fridge, I rarely stock our fridge with pop. Occasionally we ask parents to send desserts with their students to share. If we have specifically asked for sugar cookies then we supply frosting and sprinkles for decorate your own cookie night.

Worship does not equal singing. Mix up your worship with singing, scripture reading, poems, prayer, videos, small groups, joys & sorrows . . . This year we will be hosting a series called, Create in Me and will give the students the opportunity to worship through art, as we will set up an entire room as an art station.

Keep your lessons short (thirty minutes or less); even if this means stretching one lesson over a two week period. Remember, your students have been in class at school for three days by the time they get to youth group; which puts the pressure on you to be creative with your thirty minute lesson.

Plan out your lessons in short four to six week series; this helps to keep your students engaged, you from getting bogged down, and allows you to deliver information in bite-sized chunks. Be sure to promote your lessons series on your monthly and yearly calendars and newsletters. This will keep both your students and their parents informed, and will keep you on track.

To help your ministry run smoothly work with the other ministries in the church which are meeting on Wednesday nights so that all ministries line up time-wise. Our program ends at 7:30pm which is the same time that our children's program ends, thus making it easy on parents who have children in both programs. Orchestra (which is made up of mostly students) practice begins at 8:00pm, which allows our students time to hang out between youth and practice. Once a year the children's ministry (which, by the way, is called Kid K'Motion) hosts a roller skating party on a Wednesday night. We cancel Open House that week in order to join the younger kids. And when Kid K'Motion has their fall harvest party, our students volunteer to work the party, and then we host a bon fire and wiener roast afterwards.

Plan Ahead

Planning ahead is vital to running a smooth ministry. It keeps all parties informed of the direction that the ministry is heading; and by all parties I mean: your spouse, pastoral staff, board of trustees, adult volunteers, parents, and students.

There will be some annual events that are on your calendar every year. For us those events are our ski trip that we hold on the Sunday before Martin Luther King Day; summer camp that is held the second and third week in June; and state youth convention that is in early November.

Regardless of the study, event, program, outing, or fund raiser it is important to keep notes for future use. Notes need to include people, places, addresses, phone numbers, web-sites, and what to bring lists. Even though this church has been snow skiing for over twenty-five years on the same weekend at the same ski park, we keep notes, and do a review each year in order to improve on the next year's trip.

Acquire as much information about what you want to do as possible. While in Denver, Colorado for class I stopped at the brochure kiosk in my hotel lobby and collected as many cards as I could, as my youth group would be heading to Denver a year later. I still have most of those cards in a folder in my file cabinet. Acquiring information helps you build a better event, trip or program, and allows you to know the answers to questions parents and students are going to ask. Thanks to the internet acquiring information is extremely easy, and not doing so is pure and simple laziness on your part.

Promote early. As soon as you have dates, times, costs . . . begin to promote on your Face Book page, web site, in your newsletter, on your bulletin board, and verbally with your students. The sooner that parents and students get it on their calendars the better the chances are that they will make it a priority to attend.

By the middle of summer you should have your entire school year planned out, even if you do not have all the details. You should know what Wednesday nights you will not be meeting due to holidays and Kid K'Motion skating parties. You should have your lesson series planned out, not written, just the name, topic and focus of each series. You should know what annual events and big events you will be hosting and participating in. Your fundraisers should be lined up, as well as your Sunday Intenses and Super Sundays.

By early spring you should have the same done for your summer schedule.

Any big trip you plan you need to plan far in advance and be able to answer Who? What? When? Where? Why? and How? We take a cross country trip every two years, and I literally begin planning two years out, and am able to present the trip package to my students and parents ten months prior to departure. One year, as we were pulling out of Florida for the long drive back to Ohio, I began planning our next trip, and had it planned out by the time Rhonda asked me to take over driving.

For events, programs and fundraiser that you are going to repeat it is a good idea to have a tote of the needed supplies for each of these. Fill and label the tote, and store it in a safe place until needed.

Make sure you know how many volunteers you will need for each event, trip or outing, as well as the roles of those volunteers and then recruit early. Be sure to fully prepare, train and equip these volunteers for each of the different events that you use them for.

Calendar

There are three calendars that you need to create each year. The first is the one for the school year, and have it available by mid-August. This calendar should be as complete as possible, containing your Wednesday night programming (with study topics), your Sunday programming (both studies and social gatherings), annual events, fund raisers, and all other events, trips and outings. The key to this calendar is flexibility; allow wiggle room to add, subtract and change it as the school year progresses, things change, and opportunities arise.

The second calendar is for the summer months. This one should contain all of the same information that the school year calendar does, and be available by the end of April.

The third calendar should be sent out every two months with your youth newsletter. It should contain the information and details for the upcoming two months. This is when you can make needed changes and adjustments to your yearly calendar.

These calendars need to be included in the newsletter that you mail out, posted on-line, hung on your bulletin board, and posted in the youth room and in your Sunday school rooms. The more often you get your information in front of your students and their parents the better chance you will have of them remembering, and being involved.

Cutting Costs on Trips

There are a variety of ways to cut overall costs and pass the saving on to your students when going on trips.

The easy way to cut costs is to discover those people in your church who have deep and generous pockets. Once you know who these people are, pass around the opportunities to give. Warning: do not ask too many times as you do not want the money to dry up. And, although the deep pocket people are more willing to scholarship a student to summer camp or convention, sometimes they are willing to pay for pizza or to cover an entire meal for the group.

When you plan out your travel schedule try to do so in a way that you will avoid meals on the road: leave after breakfast, or arrive home before dinner. When you do have to travel during meal times, have students pack a brown bag for the road. I use this technique when we leave the church parking lot around meal times; not only does it save money, it saves us from stopping along the road. You can also buy bulk bread, peanut butter, jelly, chips, cookies and drinks and assemble brown bags while on the road. As a part of our International Youth Convention experience we spend an afternoon working on a service project. In order to save both time and money I have adults assemble brown bags and hand them to each student as they board the bus prior to our service project.

When staying in hotels and motels instead of putting four people to a room, squeeze in a fifth. Some hotels and motels offer roll away beds, and some adults and / or students are willing to sleep on the floor. Due to the growing concern of adults sharing beds with students, I volunteer to sleep on the floor in my room, which opens up bed space for a fifth male student to join us.

When traveling across America network with your sister churches that are on your travel route to stay the night in their buildings. Look for churches that have showers and kitchens; churches with gyms and couches are a simply a bonus.

On most outings you will be traveling by vehicle, which means you will need to pay for gas. One way to pay is to work the cost of gas into the fee you charge students to attend. You can ask the drivers to donate their gas. Or, even better, you can ask your board of trustees to budget funds for gas needed for youth outings, whether the gas is going into church vehicles or privately owned vehicles.

Always try to buy group tickets. If group tickets are not available, call directly and ask for a group rate. Sometimes, even when you do not have enough attendees to get the group rate, it is actually cheaper to buy the group rate and burn one or two unused tickets in order to save a few dollars; simply do the math both ways before deciding. In today's electronic media world, some on-line ticket vendors charge to mail your physical tickets, whereas you can print them off at home and save this surcharge.

Through either your youth budget, or through the deep pockets mentioned above, work it out to offer scholarships for those students who are in need. Another place to find scholarship money is in the youth accounts of students who have graduated and left money behind. I have a former student who is now in college. During his youth ministry years he was faithful to work every fundraiser. However, his parents always paid his way, thus leaving his account balance in excess of over $1000 when he graduated. He also attended summer camp, state and international youth conventions. Occasionally I contact him and give him the opportunity to scholarship a student with his left over funds. He has never told me "no".

Worship

Somewhere along the way the church re-defined the word "worship" to mean singing. With that said, I will say that today's church, being led by young, modern worship leaders, is working hard to undo what the worship leaders that came before them have done. Sadly, worship has also been restricted to only singing in our youth ministries as well. As youth leaders we must help students discover their worship language.

My friend John, who is a former youth leader and is now a year round camp director does not sing in worship, as it is not his worship language.

Though I do sing in worship, to the radio in my truck, and sometimes to my wife, I really am not a very good singer. I have never been trained beyond my seventh grade music class, I do not have a very good voice, and I can neither carry a tune nor stay on pitch. Even if I could sing, singing is not my worship language either.

However, people expect to sing during worship, and to have music played; therefore, the challenge for us is to be truly creative when we do use singing and music.

Like most contemporary churches, the church I am currently at has done away with hymnals and instead projects the words of our songs on to a screen; even in youth room we use a projector. Several years ago the projector in our youth room died and we were going to be two Wednesday nights without it. One of my senior high students, who was a traditionalist, who confessed that he missed the hymnals, who did not like to sing and usually never did, offered up a solution. He had a cd of country music star, Alan Jackson, singing hymns. For the next two weeks we used his Jackson cd, while singing out of a stack of hymnals that I had borrowed from the sanctuary. The students actually loved it, and David, the boy whose idea it was, actually sang.

Videos are literally available with the stroke of a key. You can incorporate music videos that students can either sing along to, or just watch; videos of preachers, spoken word artists, comedians, inspiration, promotion. . .

David danced naked before the Lord, so why can't we dance in youth ministry before the Lord (especially if we promise to keep our clothes on)? We use dance with some of our worship songs; and sometimes, we dance just for fun, we Interlude, Chainsaw, Cupid Shuffle, and Electric Slide.

My personal worship language is found in nature; therefore I try to incorporate nature into our youth ministry worship. We may be on a hike, a canoe trip, in the mountains, at a lake, or just on the green space at our church, but I take advantage of these places to teach and encourage my students to worship the God of creation.

David wrote many of the Psalms as worship. In fact, from Genesis to Revelations, the Bible is filled with Scripture that were written as worship to God. Instead of saving Scripture for the lesson, use it as an act of worship. Whether you or a student brings the passage, the reading of the Word is vital in worship.

So is prayer. Too many times we set prayer aside, and separate it from worship; when it truly is an important part of worship. If prayer is simply having a conversation with God, and if worship is truly about bringing praise, honor and glory to God, it make perfect sense for us to talk to Him while worshiping Him.

I have already touched on using Scripture, but there are also may wonderful pieces of literature that are not found in the Bible that can be incorporated into worship simply as a reading, such as an excerpt from a sermon, or a book; a famous quote or an inspiring story. Or the reading can be a poem. Maybe a Psalm, or one of the many other poems found in Scripture. Maybe the poem is from a famous author, or from one of your own students; maybe the poet delivers their work via video, or maybe live and on stage.

Whatever you do during worship, be creative. Discover your worship language; but more importantly, help your students discover theirs.

When my wife and I had our first child we took classes in preparation for the delivery; I still remember some of the breathing techniques that we used. I sometimes take those techniques and combine them with music, candles, or a calming scent, all to help the students to slow down and focus on God.

My intern, Emily, purchased a large puzzle that was blank of both sides. She handed a puzzle piece to each student and supplied them with markers. During our time of worship the students were instructed to draw on their pieces the blessings that God had given them recently. We then glued the puzzle together, framed it and hung it in our youth room.

More than once, during a night of worship, we have had the students remove their shoes and socks before entering the room, as the place they were about to enter was set aside as Holy Ground.

We have served communion during worship as only youth leaders can: pizza crust and Coke; hot dog buns and red punch; wafers and grape juice; loaf of bread and one cup to be passed around . . .

When we practice foot washing we always use unscented baby wipes instead of basins of water and towels.

Student Ministry Team

The Student Ministry Team that you assemble will be the reason that your youth ministry rocks (or doesn't). Make sure that the members on your team love God, and love students (in that order).

When putting your team together purposely recruit the adults you want based on what they can bring to the table, and how well they will fit with you, the team, and your students.

Some of your team members will be skilled players, as are some of mine:

- Allie—registered nurse (first aid coordinator)
- Betsy—treasurer
- Brionne—support staff and fundraisers
- Craig & Belinda—air travel coordinators
- Doug & Lulu – fundraisers, college age ministry
- Jeff & Jayna—support staff and fundraisers
- Joey—food service professional

    Other team members will be utility players:

- Bobby & Nancy—Open House volunteers, Sunday school teachers, Intense leaders, and ski trip coordinators
- Cody—Open House volunteer, Sunday school helper, chaperone
- Danny—Open House volunteer, Sunday school teacher, Intense leader, chaperone, driver
- Emily—Youth Ministry Assistant, Open House volunteer, Sunday school teacher, Intense leader

- Randy & Roxanne—Open House volunteers, Sunday school teachers, Intense leaders, support staff, chaperones, drivers
- Rhonda—Open House volunteer, Sunday school teacher, Intense leader, chaperone, driver
- Sue—Open House volunteer, Sunday school teacher, chaperone, driver
- Tania—Sunday school teacher, Intense leader, chaperone, driver, professional baker
- Todd & MeLeah—Sunday school teachers, Intense leaders, chaperones, drivers

Use your team members according to their gifts and strengths. Have those that are gifted in teaching, teach; those that are coordinators, coordinate; those that are nurses, nurse; those that have mini-vans, drive; those that cook & bake, cook & bake . . .

Regardless of their gifts and strengths, or how good they naturally are with students, train and resource them. If you can afford it take them to youth ministry conferences and seminars to aid in their training.

I once worked a deal where Danny and I were able to work for a vendor at a national youth leader's conference in exchange for our registrations being paid. I had the church cover our gas and hotel; which allowed the two of us to attend and enjoy the conference for very little cost.

Every fall I attend a one day seminar led by a national youth speaker. When Emily came on board as my assistant I began taking her along.

Every two years, at our International Youth Convention, there is a morning of youth leader training offered. I make sure that I take care of my students on this morning so that my adults can attend this training opportunity.

It is important to resource them as well as train them. Whether they are teaching a class, leading a small group, running a game, or just taking a student to dinner, it is important that you resource them with the tools they need: curriculum, sporting equipment, food, funding . . .

After you have recruited, trained, and resourced them, give them freedom to be themselves, and allow them to use their own creativity. Allowing your leaders to do so is empowering to them, and will result in you having an amazing team of awesome individuals.

Protect your team members. Give them breaks and time off. This includes limiting how many quarters they can teach in a year. Make sure that they spend time with their own families. Tell them "no" sometimes. When possible, use parents instead of team members as drivers and chaperones.

As a way of supporting them, pay for their: admission, gas, meal, parking, t-shirt . . . And throughout the year honor them, as individuals, and as a team with: dinner, dessert, outings . . . Occasionally, during our planning meetings Rhonda and I will treat our team with dessert (brownies and ice cream or ice cream floats); or we will plan our meeting at meal time and grill burgers, chicken or steak for them. The past several years I have partnered with a local minor league baseball team to buy group tickets (that include a hat and a meal) so that our team can attend a game together.

Relational Ministry

Jesus had more than just twelve disciples. People from all walks of life followed Him; however, He chose to invest in twelve. Furthermore, He intimately invested in three (known as the Inner Circle), Peter, James and John. Jesus was practicing relational ministry.

Relational ministry is not about programs, games, studies, lessons, trips, events, or anything else we seem to associate with youth ministry. Relational ministry is about having relationships with our students and helping them form, maintain and grow in their relationships with God. Ironically, we often do so through the items listed above.

I believe relational ministry happens best when we instill some of the following:

There is a huge difference between quality time and quantity time. Students want loving, caring, accepting adults to spend time with them . . . When you are doing so, make sure you are investing quality time, and not just putting in the hours. Quality one-on-one time, or small group time, is priceless to students, and will pay huge dividends as you build your youth family.

We must learn and practice the art of the long supper. Two things happen when we share a meal with others: we eat and we talk. The long supper is an intentional extension of the meal to create time for intentional conversation, which in turn builds and solidifies relationships.

We will load groups of students into our church van and drive an hour just to eat a meal together. Combining drive time and meal time these groups will spend three hours together; a lot of youth family dynamics happen in those three hours, especially when two of those hours we are locked in a van with nothing to do but sit, watch and talk.

We have a rule when riding that all electronic media devices are put away, so that students can focus on those around them. Sometimes we allow students to ride in whatever vehicle they want, so that they can be with their friends. Other times we randomly assign vehicles which forces students to begin and build relationships with those outside of their circles.

Our group happens to travel several times a year where we are required to stay in a hotel. Room assignments are crucial. The conversations, antics and bonding that happen in hotel rooms between adults and students, and students and students, is truly unique to the setting. Carefully think through your room assignments when you pair up adults and students. I believe in two different approaches: assigning rooms that will create new relationships and foster young ones; or putting people together that are already close and allowing them to bond even tighter. My advice is that you use both of these models. Most importantly, you must listen to the needs of the group. I have had adults request certain students, as they truly had a burden for them and wanted to spend the weekend with them; to stay up into the wee hours of the morning conversing and bonding.

In another chapter I shared my heart and passion on how I feel about summer camp. Spending a week in a cabin with your students is some of the best hours you will invest over the six years those students will be with you. I still carry with me camp cabin memories from when I was a camper, and some of those involve my counselors. (Like the night our counselors woke up us up in the middle of the night, took us out to the ball field and let us have an epic pillow fight; during which they snuck back to the cabin so that if we got busted they would not get in to trouble).

In recent summers my group of boys has been large enough that we require a cabin to ourselves . . . just me and fifteen junior high boys; burping, farting, guzzling Mt. Dew after midnight, talking about girls, discussing our flag football game plan, laughing, crying, sharing, and discovering God.

I am forty-two years old and have been going to camp for eighteen summers. My friend, Bryan, who is a volunteer youth leader, and who is older than me, takes a week of personal vacation to attend junior high camp with his boys in order to practice relational youth ministry, and has been for as long as I can remember.

One-on-one time is vital. Caution: only spend one-on-one time with the same gender. If you are planning on meeting with a student of the opposite gender, take along your spouse, or other trusted youth leader. Communicate with the parents when spending time with their kids and give them the answers to Who? What? When? Where? Why? and How?

When spending one-on-one time with students always pay, whether it is a meal, a movie ticket, or an admission price. Build funds for such times into your budget. One of my favorite one-on-one times revolves around Wendy's and French fries dipped in Frostys. A close second would be taking students to hole-in-the-wall restaurants and introducing them to greasy spoon cooking.

There is also a chapter concerning the importance of you being in the stands of their events, cheering them on, hugging them afterwards, and taking pictures with them. I remember as a student when a fellow student from a different high school brought his yearbook to church, and there was a picture of our youth pastor sitting on the front row watching a basketball game. Later, when I accepted my call to youth ministry, I remembered that photo and it has inspired me to sit in the stands.

Youth pastor, author and speaker, Laurie Polich, tells the story of when she and her husband moved to a new city, and to a new church. Instead of diving back into youth ministry she went to the youth group and simply observed. She soon found what she was looking for, that one girl who needed an adult in her life who would journey with her. For several years Laurie made this one girl her youth group. I believe that this story alone hammers home the importance of relational ministry.

Involve Them in Your Personal Life

If you are truly going to practice relational ministry then you must be their youth leader outside of the walls of the church. Besides attending their stuff, include them in your stuff. Whatever it is you are doing you can always involve a student, whether you are cooking, cleaning, shopping, running errands, volunteering, visiting people, working on your yard, your car, or your house.

I am an outdoorsman and have taken students boating, shooting, hunting, fishing, and hiking. Recently I taught Emily (my youth ministry assistant), and Randy and Tanner (a father and son) gun safety, followed by an afternoon of shooting targets and clay birds.

My wife, Rhonda, includes girls when cooking and baking, shopping, scrap booking, crafting, and attending plays and movies.

There is a powerful message sent when you invite students into your life outside of the church, and beyond your paycheck. You are telling them that you truly love them and that they really matter.

Service and Missions

In Matthew 28:19 we are called to go and make disciples; in Mark 12:31 we are told to love our neighbors as ourselves; in Mark 16:15 we are instructed to preach the Gospel to all nations; and in James 1:27 we are given the duty of looking after the orphans and the widows. These verses, and so many more, support the need for the church to be involved in service and missions work.

I believe that many Christians are convinced that being a full time missionary means that one will serve in a foreign land for their entire life. Sadly, there are some that believe Missions = Africa.

My oldest son, Jordan, is currently a freshman at Ohio Christian University studying Disaster Relief and Management. He feels a call on his life to serve full time in the missions field. I have witnessed firsthand his journey of discovery of this calling, as he too initially thought that being called as a missionary meant that he would serve in Africa for the rest of his life. He is taking these next four years to truly understand his call, and to explore the vast and varied opportunities that are before him as a full time missionary. This summer he joined twenty other people from our church for a week long missions trip to Honduras, where he got firsthand experience, and the realization that Missions does not always equal Africa.

Please hear my heart and understand that I am not in any way discounting the call of missions, or those that serve in full time foreign missions. I personally feel that there is an abundance of work that needs to be done locally, and countless number of people who live right where we do that need to hear the message of Christ. This morning, on my day off from the office, I partnered with several local organizations to help provide new shoes to five different school districts, meeting the needs of over 320 students.

I have worked hard to plug my students into, and make them aware of, local needs. I have also worked hard that we as a group try to meet some of these needs, as well as educating, equipping and encouraging my students to be involved in local service and missions as individuals.

Over the years we have participated in the following local missions: food drives, clothing drives, partnered with the local Red Cross to host blood drives (and my students who were old enough even donated), cut down and hauled away trees from various properties, painted walls in various homes and buildings, landscaped homes and charities, worked with the local parks department to set up and tear down city Christmas lights, volunteered hours at local food banks, storm clean-up for the elderly, senior high students have volunteered with Campus Life Middle School programs, helped run a summer lunch program, annually volunteer during Vacation Bible School, partnered with local nursing homes,

During that same time frame, we have, on a state level: been a part of the set up and tear down crew for the Ohio State Youth Convention, partnered with local ministries and charities of the host city for the Ohio State Youth Convention, senior high students have volunteered as cabin counselors during summer camp, weekend work camps at our state camp groups to prepare for summer camp, and to breakdown camp at the end of summer, and volunteered hours in the warehouse of a medical missions ministry.

Even beyond our state boundaries we: financially support a former student who now serves with Fellowship of Christian Athletes, and partner with local ministries and charities of the host city for the International Youth Convention.

On a global scale we: annually participate in the Operation Christmas Child ministry, have adopted and financially support a girl in Peru, a few of our students have gone to Peru with our missions ministry to help build a church building and to run a Vacation Bible School, and most recently, twenty-one people (most of which were college aged and two high school students) went to Honduras to build a bathroom facility, a boat dock and to run a Vacation Bible School.

I have found that in order to keep my students interested in service and missions work I need to offer them a variety of projects from hammer & nails to personal relationships. Being an outdoorsman, a wood worker and a handyman I am drawn to jobs where we build something and see the result of our work at the end of the day; however, not all of my students enjoy these projects, so I must schedule personal relationship projects as well.

Years ago a full time missionary, which was serving in downtown Atlanta, told me that true missions is simply finding a need and meeting it. I have taught and modeled this truth to my students in hopes that in their personal lives they would live missionally. I have several students who donate blood on a regular basis; one recently ran in a mud run to raise funds for breast cancer research; as I mentioned, one is serving with Fellowship of Christian Athletes; one has gone on three missions trips with other organizations; a former student, who has a painting ministry, gives a percentage of her earnings to a ministry that is working to end human trafficking, and one recently partnered with an organization to raise awareness and funds to help free child soldiers in third world countries.

My thought on service and missions is simply: do something. Be creative, have fun, work hard, serve your fellow man, and do it all in the name of Christ.

Youth Room Fridge

One of my favorite pieces of furniture in our youth room is the fridge. Besides the obvious use, storing food and drinks, we use it just like you use the one in your kitchen at home: we tape promotional flyers to it, as well as pictures from past events.

To help with these ads that we have strategically placed, we keep the fridge well stocked with drinks, and we never set them out, instead the students have to open the fridge door to get their beverage, thus forcing them to see our flyers.

In my previous church, we did not have a fridge, so instead, I took the door off of one, built a wooden frame for it, and mounted it to the wall. Again, we used it as a place to put our promotional flyers and sign-ups.

This Guy Missed the Point

A guy I graduated from college with, who after graduation, spent many years church hoping from youth ministry to youth ministry posted this self-description on his Face Book page: Funny looking, spends too much time on my iPhone, does Geocaching with my kids and tries to do student ministries without getting hurt.

Now, I agree, he is funny looking, and he is a technology geek, so he probably is on his phone too much; but his comment about trying to do student ministry without getting hurt has always bothered me.

Youth ministry is truly about giving your life away. It is about journeying alongside and doing life with students. Hurt and pain are a part of this ministry. Students will hurt you and disappoint you. And even if they don't, they will hurt and suffer pain, and as their youth leaders, we must hurt with them, walk with them, and even help them carry their pain.

Instead of trying not to get hurt, just know that it is going to happen; but hurting with your students is worth it, and will impact them more than most of will ever know or realize.

For the times that they do hurt us, remember, Jesus was hurt by His disciples, too. Think about Peter, His right-hand man, who denied him three times; or Judas who sold him out for thirty pieces of silver. And when they do hurt you, turn it into a teaching moment of God's love, mercy, grace and forgiveness.

Continue Your Education

Regardless of your level of education, you need to continue that education as long as you are in ministry.

I have never understood how it is that teachers are required to continue their education (here in Ohio they are required to earn a master's degree), and doctors are required to log so many hours of education and training each year. Yet, youth leaders are not; and we work in a field that is ever changing and constantly being influenced by culture.

Continued education must include: reading good youth ministry related books; attending seminars and conferences; conversing with other youth leaders; logging on to youth ministry web sites; following quality youth leaders; staying up on culture and technology; visiting other youth ministries; and taking classes at a college or university.

I have a favorite author that I read, as well as favorite websites that I visit. Whenever I attend another church I always make it to their youth room, grab any written material they have, and pick the leaders brains. My undergrad is in Specialized Ministries with an emphasis on Youth (forgive them, it was 1995 and few schools were offering a degree in youth ministry). Fourteen years into my ministry I began working on a Masters in Youth Ministry, which I earned in 2012. Now, I am contemplating what my doctorate will be in. Regardless, I need to continue my youth ministry education, as do you.

Sex

I truly, deeply, honestly believe that the two most important decisions a person will make is their response to Jesus Christ, and whom they will marry.

Sex plays a huge role in the lives of our students, and we have a very limited time (six to seven years) to educate them with both Biblical and practical wisdom for their current and future sexual decisions.

Since entering youth ministry nineteen years ago I have set aside the month of February to talk about sex, I call it L.S.D. (love, sex and dating). All parties involved, my church, my adults, students and their parents, both love February, and hate it. Regardless, we must, and we will, deal with the issues of love, sex and dating.

Creativity is the key when making a topic an annual event. Regardless of which aspect, love, sex or dating, you are talking about, approach it from a different angle each year.

I have covered the topic of love from the following angles: teaching the three Greek loves: philos, eros, agape; journeying from crushin' to puppy love to real love; a study on Biblical couples; debating the world view vs the church view on love; and as a Scriptural study. You can and must apply the same creativity to sex and dating as well.

As you plan your studies on love, sex and dating, be sensitive to your students and to the subjects. We regularly divide our students by gender, or by age during the month of February. Sometimes we keep them together, but not very often.

Communicate with your parents so that they are aware of what you will be teaching. Open the doors for them to sit in your meetings. Encourage them to follow up each week with their own students. And be understanding, whether you agree or not, if they choose to keep their students home during February.

Incorporate health care professionals from within your church. We regularly rely on the nurses, doctors and professional counselors in our church to help us. The benefit is that they are able to present the information from a health care view, yet maintain Christian values and standards. It also opens doors of communication between students and those health care professionals for future, private conversations.

Elsewhere in this book I have written about our one night only event where Dr. Matt and Nurse Chad joined the guys, and Nurses Chris and Allie, and Counselor MeLeah joined the girls. During the guys only event I had a few questions prepared for Matt and Chad, and we allowed the boys to write down questions that they had concerning puberty, girls, and sex. Out of those questions stemmed some great discussions. Even though Matt and Chad do not serve on my youth ministry team, they have begun a relationship with my boys where my students now know Matt and Chad are good, safe, Godly men that they can seek out when they have personal questions about themselves, their bodies, girls, and sex.

The best advice I can offer when it comes to tackling the subjects of love, sex and dating is to understand that it is not a one-and-done lesson or conversation. These need to be continual conversations during their time in youth ministry, during their college and young adult lives; and even into their marriages. I have had many conversations with former students, who are dating, engaged or married, about love and sex.

Be transparent. Yes, sex may be uncomfortable to talk about, but it is vitally important that we do talk about it. Remember, if you are married, then you are having sex. You have the experiences of love, sex and dating to draw on. Share with your students the good and bad, the joys and sorrows, the pleasures and pains of love, sex and dating.

I go back to how I started this chapter that marriage is the second most important decision we as humans will make. Do your best to prepare your students for this life changing choice, and all that comes with it.

Utilize Technology

I have to preface this chapter by confessing that I, personally, am not a huge fan of technology. I only have an iPhone because my other phone died and I got a great deal on this one. Truth be known, if I could, I would have most of the stuff taken off my phone; I just need to call and text, and the camera is nice. However, I understand that we live in a technology driven culture, and our students have mass amounts of technology literally at their fingertips. Therefore, though I do not embrace technology, I do utilize it (to the best of my abilities).

Depending upon the size of your church, your youth group, and your budget either build and maintain a website, or use a few pages on your church's website. Our church has a pretty simple website, yet it affords me to dedicate several pages to my youth ministry (and I do not have to pay anything out of my youth budget).

Currently, it seems that everyone is on Face Book. Since most of your students, and their parents, are on Face Book, build and maintain a youth ministry page. Most likely you already have a personal page, so you know how to build one; and Face Book is free.

Most of your students also have a cell phone and they text. Sending mass text to your students, parents and adults is a simple, effective way to communicate.

Like snail mail, e-mail is slowly going the way of the buffalo among our students; however, most of their parents still maintain an e-mail account, making mass e-mails still an effective way to communicate.

Though I am not a tweeter, my students are. For those of you who do tweet, it is, again, another great way to communicate.

Besides using technology to communicate we must incorporate it in to our meeting times. Whether we are using videos from

YouTube, Skyping, running Power Point, or working with Media Shout or Pro Presenter, it benefits us, our students and our meetings when we use technology.

Most Wednesday nights our announcements are given through a Power Point slide show. Sometimes, depending on my lesson, I will also use Power Point slides to visualize my points. During worship I use videos, Pro Presenter and Power Point.

Technology is ever changing, and that is not a bad thing. Utilizing technology is not a bad thing either, especially when our students are already submersed in it. If, like me, you are not a huge fan of technology, instead of bucking it, find the techo-nerd in your youth ministry to build, run and maintain all of your technology needs.

Remember to go old school on occasion. Turn off the cell phones, unplug technology, go outside, worship with an acoustic guitar, and lead a lesson straight from the Bible. If you really want to go old school, pull out the flannel graphs.

Background Checks

Regardless if you are a youth leader at a small church made up of mostly related family members, or you serve at a mega-church of 25,000, you must background check all of the adults who will be working alongside you and with your students.

Furthermore, your church should background check all of the people who will be working with students of any age from the nursery to seniors in high school; whether they are a Sunday school teacher, a Wednesday night leader, or only volunteer once a year in the summer for Vacation Bible School.

Background checks can be done through your local sheriff's office or through a variety of other agencies that you can find on-line. Regardless of how you choose to background check your people there will be a cost, which will either need to be a line item in the budget, or left up to the individual to pay.

If a volunteer has only lived in your state for less than three to five years I strongly suggest expanding their background check from a statewide to a nationwide.

Along with doing background checks I strongly suggest training all of your volunteers to be aware of, and be able to identify, signs of child neglect and abuse. This can be done though a curriculum, a dvd based curriculum, or through a trained professional.

In addition to both of these, and even though you should have a health care professional on your youth ministry team, it is also a good idea to make sure that your team is trained in basic first aid. I strongly suggest that this be taught by a trained professional, and refreshed every few years.

Local Schools

It is important that you partner with the local school system, or with the schools that feed your ministry. Some schools are very open to youth leaders coming in, while some are closed to the idea.

Being a small town, Eaton has only one junior high and one high school (in fact, both schools sit on the same campus, and are physically connected). However, there are five high schools in Preble County, of which four currently feed my ministry. Since moving here ten years ago the Eaton schools, as well as the county schools, have been very open to my presence.

For five years a local youth pastor and I partnered with several area businessmen and women to fully fund an all-county youth rally that was hosted at one of the schools, rotating schools each year.

In recent years Youth for Christ has moved in to Eaton, and we are now working with them to do a newer version of that youth rally. Y.F.C. has also started a Friday morning junior high campus life that I volunteer at, which puts me in the junior high every Friday morning for twenty minutes, working, hanging and playing with the 100+ sixth, seventh and eighth graders that attend.

During the football season our family life center is the site of the team's Thursday night dinner. The entire team, trainers, cheerleaders and coaches gather in our building after practice for a high carb meal. I make it a point to stand at the door and greet each person that walks in, then I bring up the end of the line and either sit with some of my students, or with the senior players.

Rhonda and I attend countless sporting events, concerts, competitions and award ceremonies during the school year, and we make it a point to say hello to the coaches, the band director, the teachers who are in charge, the principle, or the super-intendant, as a way of letting them know that we are in support of both our students and their schools.

My longevity here in Eaton, along with the relationship that I have built with the schools has opened several doors of ministry for me. I have been a guest speaker in a high school biology classroom to discuss the Biblical view on human sexuality. I have been a presenter during career day to talk about ministry. I was appointed to a special task force that worked with the board of education to help push a tax levy through. I am the pastoral advisor, and Rhonda is the official muffin baker, for the Friday morning prayer group that meets before school. But the opportunity that I love the most, and look forward to every year is the time I get to spend with Coach Burnett's freshman gym class.

Let me start by telling you that I grew up with roller skates attached to my feet. There was a rink a mile down the road from my house. Every Friday night my brother and I could be found there; and if we scraped and saved enough money during the week, we would be there on Saturday nights too. During the summers we were there every session that the rink was open. And in high school my very first job was working for a skating rink.

Every January our Children's Director hosts an all-church skating party at the rink in the neighboring town of Richmond. I have always partnered with the Children's Ministry, and moved youth group to the rink so that my students can go skating. Many years ago Coach Burnett and his wife (who attend my church) attended the skating party and he watched me on my wheels. The following Sunday he pulled me aside and asked if I would be interested in joining him and his freshman gym class for their two week session on roller skating. The next day I asked my senior pastor for the time away, and thankfully, he saw the opportunity for ministry, and allowed me the two weeks away from the office. I have been skating with the freshman gym class for seven years now.

It is awesome when a student, who I do not know, sees me in public and talks to me about skating in gym class; it is even better when a parent is with them and I get to introduce myself as a local youth pastor. It is also pretty cool when I attend graduation and lean over to Rhonda to let her know that I taught a lot of those kids how to skate.

Through these partnerships with the schools, I have been able to start and build relationships with students. Some do end up coming to Wednesday night youth group, but most I just see out in public, or at school functions. Regardless, it is a good thing when the girl who is making my sandwich at Subway is one that I taught to skate; or the boy waiting my table at Buffalo Wild Wings is a former football player that I fist-bumped every Thursday night for four years; or the girl that graduated from Huntington University with her Bachelor's Degree at the same ceremony in which I earned my Master's Degree connects with me because we are the only two students graduating from Eaton, Ohio, and during our conversation remembers attending those all-county youth rallies.

Ministry does not always happen in our youth rooms, or in our churches; in fact, some of the best ministry happens on the student's turf, where they feel comfortable. By me coming to their gym class, to their team dinner, to their place of employment, and by them knowing that I am a youth pastor, that I love God, and that I am loving them creates some of the best ministry moments.

Boy / Girl Safety

When working with boys and girls their safety has to be your number one priority.

Regardless of the event, trip, or outing you must have a proper adult to student ratio, and furthermore, you must have male and female chaperones if you have male and female students participating.

You must never allow your students or your adults to be put into a situation where they are alone with a person of the opposite gender.

We all have that one student who is the last to be picked up, or who always needs a ride home. On more than one occasion I have had to ask one of my female adults to wait around, or give a female student a ride home.

When a female student wants to talk with me, I give them the choice of either Rhonda joining us, or picking one of my female team members to talk with instead.

Even when the event is guys only or girls only, you must take precautions by having enough adults, and by keeping things open and in the public.

When it comes to staying in hotels and motels more and more student ministries are re-thinking how they set up room assignments when travelling; some are putting two adults and two students in a room, some are putting one adult and two students in a room, some are going with no adults in a room, some are only booking suites that can sleep five to six people. Regardless of their rooming assignments, they are trying to not put an adult in a bed with a student.

The best offense to the safety of our students is to educate and train both your adults and your students; furthermore, to be transparently honest about your expectations during events, trips and outings. Sometimes, though, life happens, and you have to deal with it the best you can. When life does put you or your ministry in a tough situation be sure that you either document the events well, or talk with someone about the situation during and after.

Case in point, years ago while at summer camp I had a former student who was in college and serving on staff as the nurse. The week before camp Krista was in a four-wheeler accident and required several stitches on her upper inner thigh. During the first week of camp her incision became infected and she needed to go to the hospital. Due to the fact that our staff was shorthanded already, I, being her youth pastor, was asked by the camp director to drive Krista to the hospital, in the dark, an hour away. I made sure that both Rhonda and Krista's mom knew of our trip to the hospital before we left, and talked with them the next morning as well.

At the hospital the doctors informed us that they were going to have to re-open her wound, clean out the infection and then sew her back up. Because of the intimate area of her wound, I did not go into the procedure room with her.

When we returned to camp in the wee morning hours I woke the camp director up to let him know we had returned. That morning I met with the camp director, and had phone conversations with both Rhonda and Krista's mom to debrief them all on how the evening went. It was not the best situation to be put in, but sometimes life trumps our best intentions and we have to be willing to bend our own safety rules for the safety of others.

Hugs and I Love You

I know the pervious chapter was about being safe when working with boys and girls; but that does not trump the fact that our students want, desire, and need human touch. Creating human touch is vital when creating a youth family and when running a relational youth ministry.

Here are some safe ways to touch students: bring back the high-five, fist-bump it and blow it up, pat them on the back, squeeze them on the shoulder, and hug them.

Yes. Hug them. Just be careful, safe, and smart about it. Have a rule of same gender hugs between your adults and students. When there are cross-gender hugs make sure they are side-to-side, are in public, and kept short.

In addition to hugging your students, tell them you love them. In my twenty years of ministry I have discovered that too many of our students are not hearing "I love you"; or they are not hearing it enough. There is immeasurable power in those three words. If you really want to change a student's life, if you really want to be a Christ-like youth leader then tell your students that you love them. They may know Jesus loves them, but they need to hear and experience it.

This was all made very clear to me many years ago as I was sitting in an arena with 6000 students and leaders. Reggie Dabbs was on stage, and he came to a point in his sermon where he asked, by a show of hands, how many people need a hug right now. Hands all over the room shot up. Then he pointed to a student and called them up on stage. I watched as this student melted in the arms of love as Reggie wrapped them up and hugged them. If a total stranger can impact a student in that way, imagine what you can do with your students, the ones you are investing in, journeying with, and doing life with.

Closing Thoughts

Thank you for reading my book. I truly hope that you learned something, and that you can apply it to your ministry. I also hope that it was good enough that you will pass your copy on to a youth ministry friend.

I really do believe that Christianity can be summed up in five words: Love God and Love Others. I also believe that youth ministry needs to be kept simple . . . love your students, journey with them, and help them fall in love with Jesus.

Years ago an elderly man in my first church gave me an old piece of slate that had been painted with the words "Tell the kids I love them, God". That is our job; and I love my job.

May God bless you as you give your life away to your students.

Your Brother in Ministry,

Jeremy

Biography

Pastor Jeremy Halstead is a native of Wichita, Kansas. In 1991 he married his high school sweetheart, Rhonda (Martin). They moved to Oklahoma City, Oklahoma where he attended Mid America Bible College. In February of 1995 Jeremy and Rhonda were blessed with a son, Jordan (19). In May of that same year Jeremy graduated with a Bachelor of Arts in Specialized Ministries with an emphasis in Youth Ministry. They soon moved to Alliance, Ohio where he served as the Pastor of Student Ministries for the First Church of God for eight years. In 1997 they were blessed with a second son, Justin (17). In 2003 the family moved to Eaton, Ohio where Jeremy is currently serving as the Pastor of Student Ministries. In May of 2012 he graduated from Huntington University with a Master of Youth Ministries degree.

During his time in Ohio he has served on the Ohio State Youth Board of the Church of God for eighteen years, and has volunteered at Camp Marengo (the Ohio State Summer Camp of the Church of God) for eighteen years, serving as a cabin counselor, camp pastor, teacher, support staff and even dish washer.

Appendix A
First Aid Kit Supplies
(based on fifty people)

Alcohol Swabs
Aleo Vera
Anti-Diarrheal
Antibiotic Ointment
Benadryl
Chap Stick
Cough Drops
Gas X
Glucose Tablets
Ibuprofen
Menstrual Complete
Peppermints
Pepto-Bismol
Peroxide
Tums

Baby Wipes
Baggies
Cotton Balls
Cotton Swabs
Emergency Blanket
Hot / Cold Pads
Pen

Arm Sling
Band Aids
Gauze
Non-Stick 1st Aid Pads
Self-Adhering Bandage
Trauma Dressing
Waterproof Tape

Contacts Case
Saline Solution

Blood Pressure Cuff
Pocket Mask
Rubber Gloves
Safety Pins
Scissors
Thermometer & Covers
Tweezers

Pads
Tampons

Appendix B
Parental Consent Form

Activity _____

Name _____

Birth Date _____

Address _____

Phone (_____)_____

City _____

State _____   Zip _____

School _____

Grade in / Just completed _____

The undersigned does hereby give permission for our (my) child, _____, to attend and participate in activities sponsored by the Eaton First Church of God on 1/1/2013.

We (I) authorize an adult, in whose care the minor has been entrusted, to consent to any X-ray examination, anesthetic, medical, surgical or dental diagnosis or treatment, and hospital care, to be rendered to the minor under the general or special supervision and on the advice of any physician or dentist licensed under the provision of the Medical Practice Act on the medical staff of a licensed hospital, whether such diagnosis or treatment is rendered at the office of said physician or at said hospital.

The undersigned shall be liable and agree(s) to pay all costs and expenses incurred in connection with such medical and dental services rendered to the aforementioned child pursuant to this authorization.

Should it be necessary for our (my) child to return home due to medical reasons or otherwise, the undersigned shall assume all transportation costs.

The undersigned does also hereby give permission for our (my) child to ride in any vehicle designated by the adult in whose care the minor has been entrusted while attending and participating in activities sponsored by the Eaton First Church of God.

_____

Participant Signature   Date

_____

Parent / Legal Guardian   Date

Insurance Company   _____

Policy Number   _____

Insurance Co Phone   _____

Date of last tetanus shot   _____

Physician's name and number   _____

Dentist's name and number   _____

Bibliography

New International Version. [Colorado Springs]: Biblica, 2011.
BibleGateway.com. Web. 3 Mar. 2011.

www.ingramcontent.com/pod-product-compliance
Lightning Source LLC
Chambersburg PA
CBHW070504090426
42735CB00012B/2673